Thrive in Color

Thrive in Color

HOW TO MASTER
SELF-ADVOCACY AND
COMMAND YOUR CAREER
AS AN UNDERREPRESENTED
PROFESSIONAL

DEVIKA BRIJ

Hardcover ISBN: 978-1-955811-73-6
Paperback ISBN: 978-1-955811-65-1
E-book ISBN: 978-1-955811-66-8
LCCN: 2024900902

First hardcover edition: May 2024

Author photo: Erica J. Simmons / www.ericajsimmons.com
Cover artwork: Adil Bouimama via AdobeStock
Cover design, layout, and typesetting: Bryna Haynes
Editors: Bryna Haynes, Paul Baillie-Lane

Published by WorldChangers Media
PO Box 83, Foster, RI 02825
www.WorldChangers.Media

This book is dedicated to you, reader.

You are worthy of the "more" you desire in your professional life.

Thank you for investing the time and attention to learn the strategies in this book, and for trusting me to be a small part of your career journey.

Despite the obstacles and challenges we experience as professionals of color, together, we will thrive.

I'm excited for you.

Praise

"*Thrive in Color* displays the benefits of vulnerability, courage, resilience, and mentorship. Devika does a great job channeling the lived experiences of people of color for good. The reader is left with action plans to control the controllable within corporate structures. Success is repeated in the book when talented professionals leave where they are tolerated to discover places where they can be celebrated. The spirit of the written word allows us to believe the answer is within reach and the importance of continuously thriving for full representation and inclusion."

- Michelle Gethers, Chief Diversity Officer and Head of Corporate Responsibility, Visa

"*Thrive in Color* equips you with the essential resources to foster personal and professional growth, enabling a successful career evolution. Through its practical and strategic guidance, this book empowers you to unlock your full potential, shaping the fulfilling career you've always envisioned."

- Jabari Hearn, Managing Partner, AKQA Los Angeles

"*Thrive in Color* does something rare: it gives underrepresented professionals the inspiration and practical tools to go from feeling like passengers inside systems not designed for them to being drivers of their own career journey."

- Kofi Amoo-Gottfried, Chief Marketing Officer, DoorDash

"*Thrive in Color* offers a vital roadmap for professionals of color navigating the complexities of today's workplace. Through powerful personal anecdotes and strategic guidance, Devika addresses the challenges of bias and unfair treatment head-on, offering invaluable insights on reclaiming control of one's career narrative. Her approach empowers individuals to assert their professionalism confidently, navigate biases, and communicate effectively, fostering resilience and self-advocacy. This book isn't just about surviving; it's a guide to thriving in environments where underrepresented professionals often feel marginalized, making it an essential read for those aiming not just for success, but for ownership and empowerment in their careers."

- Diana Luu, Canada Country Manager, LinkedIn

"*Thrive in Color* brilliantly explores the pivotal shift from a defeated mindset to an enabled one, where people of color learn about the tangible tools necessary to take control of their careers. It is a must-read for those seeking accountability, empowerment, and agency over their careers."

- Sonya Kay George, Vice President of Global Strategic Accounts, Great Place to Work

"*Thrive in Color* is a must-read for anyone looking to excel in their career or seeking to understand how to navigate the complexities of the modern workplace. Through a lens that uniquely understands the challenges faced by people of color in the workplace, this book offers invaluable advice to overcome bias, imposter syndrome, and systemic barriers, and empowers people of color to boss up and fully own their career trajectory. In a world where diversity, equity, and inclusion initiatives and commitments continue to be deprioritized, this book is timely and necessary for professionals of color to stay included and thrive!"

- Shaina Poulard, Global Head of DEI, NerdWallet

"Devika Brij is a masterful teacher. I've leveraged her expertise to support underrepresented employees during my former role as Head of Diversity and Inclusion for the U.S. Banks business at Morgan Stanley and now as Head of Diversity, Equity and Inclusion at the premier digital platform for luxury fashion in North America. Our employees from diverse communities have expressed that the knowledge and tools Devika provides are some of the best they've received! Her work in mastering self-advocacy has been uplifting for the communities I lead and support in my role, and personally as a Black woman and Senior Executive in my everyday life. *Thrive in Color* is a brilliant, prescriptive guide to career success that will help professionals of color accelerate the hard career lessons that most only learn through years of trial and error."

- Dr. Alicia Williams, VP of Diversity, Equity and Inclusion, Saks

"*Thrive in Color* stands as an indispensable lifeline for professionals of color grappling with the intricacies of today's workplace. In the absence of sufficient resources or guidance, individuals of color are often left to confront the challenges of bias, marginalization, and isolation on their own. Devika's wisdom is a beacon in navigating the complexities of a workplace that may not always recognize the unique struggles faced by professionals of color. This book is not just a guide; it's a rallying cry for those committed to contributing to the success of people of color in the workplace."

- Arvin Patel, Chief Licensing Officer, New Segments, Nokia

"Devika Brij is a powerhouse voice when it comes to self-advocacy and career progression, especially for people of color. She is both inspiring and empowering while still providing tactical, real-world advice to help underrepresented professionals thrive. In a world where climbing the corporate ladder and achieving the career you desire feels increasingly difficult, Devika provides the knowledge and tools to help you reach your goals."

- Andrea Johnson, Director of Customer Success, Glassdoor

"Devika's pragmatic yet strategic approach delivers the tools you need to grow, develop, and advance in your career. As a result, I was able to accomplish the challenging career pivot that I was seeking in less than a year and increase my base salary by 30 percent. This book will help you reach your full potential and create the career you always dreamed of."

- Mena Mahaniah, Global Brand Marketing Director,
Timberland, a VF Company

Table of Contents

Introduction

MOST PEOPLE IN MY LIFE today know me as Devika Brij, CEO and Founder of Brij the Gap and consultant to companies like Visa, Meta, Glassdoor, Reddit, Converse, Morgan Stanley, and more. But before that, I was Devika Brij, marketing, HR, and sales professional across companies like Sony Music Entertainment, Google, LinkedIn, and several others. While I've been blessed to have a successful career working at highly sought-after companies, I'd be lying to you if I said it was all rainbows and butterflies. Some of my challenges were the same as those faced by any young professional, but others—the majority, if I'm being honest—were specific to being a person of color and a first-generation immigrant.

I clearly recall the moment when I realized the decision-makers around me were leading with bias, and that the systems of the corporate world were not going to work in my favor.

I was two years out of university when I took a job as a Human

Resources Coordinator with a major entertainment-tech company. My manager and my peers loved me, and I received consistent feedback about my commitment to go above and beyond to ensure that everyone I supported was winning. As a result, I doubled down on performance. If I was known to be a hard worker, I reasoned, promotions and opportunities would come to me more easily. (I'm sure you've heard that one before!)

About a year into that role, an opening came up on another team within the Human Resources department. The woman who currently held this position—let's call her Olivia—was expecting her first child and had no plans to return from her maternity leave. This role was in the recruiting function and would transition me from my current back-end systems work to a more action-oriented, customer-facing position. I was beyond excited. This promotion would allow me to thrive in ways I had already proven in my twelve months with the company: namely, my ability to work well with people, meet deadlines through an overflow of critical priorities, and help leaders make decisions that would impact the overall success of the company.

Being successful in business was important to me. I actually hadn't planned, growing up, to enter the corporate world; I studied English and education in college with the intention of becoming a high school teacher. However, on the first day of my master's program at Santa Clara University, I decided that path wasn't for me, and threw myself into the business world. I knew I'd have a large learning curve, and doing well made me feel empowered—which was how I ended up in a position for this promotion.

Immediately, several individuals across the HR function approached me. "Devika, you'd *better* interview for this role. You'd kill it!" My manager, someone I respect to this day, also encouraged me to apply. The best part was, I knew they were right.

I could do this. In fact, I couldn't *not* do this.

Three rounds of interviews later, my colleague and recruiter for that role, whom I'll call Kelsey, asked me to meet her in the boardroom. I'll never forget her beaming smile as she sang my praises and dramatically built up to the big announcement:

"Devika, you got the job!"

I felt on top of the world. This was one of the moments I'd dreamed of as a young professional: my peers and leaders recognizing the importance of my contribution and rewarding me for my efforts. I felt like this moment was the culmination of many months of learning to believe in myself, conquering the learning curve, and earning the respect of my colleagues. I had spent so long feeling lost in that job, having to figure things out on my own without any training or experience in this area of the corporate world. This offer made me feel like I truly belonged in this world—like I could set aside my imposter syndrome and claim the full impact of my accomplishments.

Then, I saw the offer letter.

Specifically, I saw the salary.

What Kelsey didn't know was that Olivia and I had had lunch together before I interviewed for the role. I'd asked her about the best and worst parts of the role. She kept it real and had been transparent about her compensation. (This wasn't a surprise, as one of my responsibilities in my current role was inputting every single employee's salary into the HR system.)

The total compensation I was offered was $10,000 more than my current entry-level salary—but still over $30,000 less than Olivia, a white woman, had been earning when she resigned. Sure, she had a few more years of experience than I did, but the role itself wasn't all that strategic. A few weeks of training would be enough to prepare me to operate successfully in that position. Plus, I already knew the internal systems, protocols, and culture, which would enable me to ramp up faster than an external hire.

I had expected to be offered $5,000, or even $10,000, under what Olivia was making. But this offer would in no way compensate me fairly for the work I'd be doing. In fact, it was $15,000 less than the minimum budget allocated for this role.

My elation turned to shock, and then disappointment. "Are they serious?" I wondered, trying not to let my disbelief show in my expression. I was young and eager, but even as an early-stage professional who was more flexible, I knew I was being taken advantage of and I wasn't having any of it.

"Thanks for your enthusiasm, Kelsey," I told her, "but there's no way I can accept this offer. You know I want this position—and since we're cross-functional peers, you know my quality of work. Is there anything I can do to get this evaluated further?"

Kelsey's face went from enthusiasm to empathy in a flash. "I totally get it, Devika. I'd feel exactly like you do right now. Let me take this back to the team and see what we can do."

I left the office that Friday afternoon feeling blindsided and confused. Still, I remained optimistic. Maybe this was just how salaries were negotiated at this level, and I needed to play hardball to prove my worth.

By Monday afternoon, I got another chat message from Kelsey, asking me to meet in the boardroom. The news wasn't good.

"We want to offer you this role," Kelsey said, "but Eleanor [the Head of the HR and Recruiting function] can only offer you $3,000 more."

Knowing Kelsey's hands were tied, I decided to ask my current manager, and the manager of the role I would be moving into, to advocate for me with Eleanor. This approach felt highly uncomfortable, but to accept the offer I needed a better solution.

Eleanor's response? "Tell her to take it or leave it."

Gutted and embarrassed, I could only say, "Thanks for trying, Kelsey, but I'm going to have to pass."

The thing that bothered me most was that I knew the next hire for the role I'd turned down would be external. Eleanor would end up offering that individual a salary within, or even over, the established budget—and that person would take six months or more to acclimate to the company.

It wasn't that Eleanor *couldn't* offer me the salary the role commanded. It was that she didn't want to.

How, I wondered, could one person make me feel so small, so undervalued, when everyone else was singing my praises? More, how could I continue to work at a company where the executive teams didn't value or fairly incentivize employees enough for them to want to stay? This was my first lesson in the fact that every company's primary goal is profit, and that they will always aim to get more for less.

A few months and several applications later, I was offered a position with a global tech giant. I was ecstatic. Growing up in Silicon Valley, an invitation to work at this company was the dream for just about everyone who wanted a career in tech. My meals and transportation to and from the office, among other amazing perks, were included in my compensation package, not to mention the salary was more than twice what I was currently making.

Until that experience, I wouldn't have believed someone if they'd told me, "It's going to be different for you as a person of color." I truly thought that the cutting-edge corporation I'd been working for would be further along in terms of equity and inclusion, that my experience as a professional of color would be different than those of my older family and friends, and that my enthusiasm, skills, and dedication would supersede any lingering biases or inequities. Unfortunately, that wasn't the case.

The challenges mounted as I progressed in my career. You'd expect that, working at some of the world's largest global companies, there would be greater opportunities for people of color, but the opposite was true. The intent was there, but the action was often missing. Even the most well-known and desirable companies have their shortcomings. The environment was highly competitive and filled with politics. Everyone was grinding to be recognized as a top performer. Whenever a role opened up, people's demeanors would change. Individuals who were normally collaborative and pleasant became competitors when it came time to secure in-demand opportunities.

I quickly learned that, to win the game, I had to become the best player. I invested in career coaches and attended dozens of seminars and workshops. After each talk or session, I would leave feeling highly motivated. However, when I got back to the office, eager to apply my new knowledge, I lacked the "how-to." Over time, I discovered that no coach or training could give me the exact formula to break through my challenges around self-advocacy, build my professional brand, and engage in meaningful ways in pursuit of my goals—partly because a lot of motivational information is about feeling, and not action, and partly because none of the people leading these workshops could relate to the experience of being a person of color in a highly competitive work space. Their strategies weren't created to address the unique challenges I was facing as an underrepresented professional.

So, I began making my own observations, and blending them with the information I was learning. I began buying lunch for people who were thriving in their careers to learn how they were doing it. Through my research, observations, and personal experiences, I created a professional development framework that would take me from entry-level individual contributor to people leader in less than six years and increase my income six times over. I consistently achieved promotions and raises, even outside of company-mandated performance reviews. I did it my way—and it worked.

My peers, particularly my peers of color, took notice. "Devika, you've been here for a fraction of the time I have. How are you getting promoted so quickly? Can you help me?" Of course, I shared what I was learning. Despite my intense travel schedule, I spent hours each week mentoring my peers. One by one, they began to drive success in ways they never imagined.

The gratification I felt at seeing their successes was immense. But at the same time, my own career was going off the rails. In 2017, I was unjustly fired from a role due, in part, to my managers' biases (a story I'll share with you later in this book). This truly devastated me and prompted me to reflect even more deeply on the strategies I was employing as a person of color working with mostly white teams. I saw where I had gone wrong, and also where I had done all I could. After taking some time away to regain my physical and mental health, I took a new role at a new company where I was making bank as a sales manager. However, given what I had faced in that previous role, and what I still saw my peers contending with, it all felt a bit … hollow. Two months into this new job, I decided to leave corporate for good—and Brij the Gap Consulting was born.

Today, I'm honored to spend my days teaching and advising people just like me—underrepresented professionals with a driving desire to advance in their chosen fields. I work with people across all industries, geographies, functions, and seniorities to offer proven strategies for career advancement so they can be empowered to create the career they deserve. I partner with some of the world's most recognized brands to develop, advance, and increase retention of underrepresented employees. I also work closely with people leaders to ensure they are building productive and empowered teams and creating pathways for employees of color by helping them understand the challenges those employees may be facing.

My corporate career was a huge learning experience—and, as challenging as it was at times, I know that it prepared me to do this vital work.

DEFINING "UNDERREPRESENTED"

We all know that systematic disadvantages exist in corporate environments and inhibit Black, Latino, Indigenous, African, Indian, Asian, and other non-white professionals from achieving equal access, opportunities, and resources compared to their peers. This shows up in many ways—unequal pay, working with unaware or openly biased leaders, less frequent advancement opportunities, unfair treatment ... the list goes on.

While recent strides in the Diversity, Equity, and Inclusion (DEI) space have started to improve outcomes for underrepresented professionals, we still have a long way to go. More, each unique group of individuals has their own set of challenges to address and overcome. For example, the experience of Black Americans is unique among marginalized groups and differs from that of recent Black immigrants or Black people living outside of North America, even though all groups are considered Black. Obviously, someone from Thailand, Egypt, or India—or someone like me, who is of mixed heritage and often described as "racially ambiguous"—will have a vastly different experience of workplace bias and limitation than a Black person of any background. However, there are key challenges that most, if not all, professionals from marginalized groups have in common—and it is those commonalities I have chosen to address in this book.

To represent the vast segment of the global population who are experiencing these adversities, I needed a term that would both honor individuals' unique experiences and also encompass our collective challenges and goals. I have chosen to use the terms "underrepresented professionals" and "professionals of color."

Professionals of color *are* hugely underrepresented. Not in the population—as many have pointed out, people of color are the majority on the planet, and are not, in fact, "minorities" at all. But we are underrepresented in leadership. Underrepresented in management. Underrepresented in client-facing roles. Underrepresented in decision-making. Underrepresented in industries that influence and impact the majority of the human race—like banking, investment, finance, media, energy, healthcare, and food production.

Landing on a term that felt appropriate was a long process, and not one I undertook lightly. I understand that preferred and appropriate terminology is always evolving—in fact, it may evolve in the period between the writing of this introduction and the release of this book!—and that as an individual you may have distinct preferences for how you are identified. It is my hope that you can feel seen and validated under the umbrellas of "underrepresented professionals" and "professionals of color," and that these collective terms leave room for your individual experience to permeate and influence your journey to success.

YOU DESERVE MORE

As a person of color, a Black individual, or a member of a culturally marginalized group, you are worthy of consistent career opportunities, open doors, leadership positions, flexibility to prioritize what you're most passionate about, and a salary that reflects your value.

I'm here to help you reach this exact vision in your professional career—the same vision that the closest people around you told you *not* to expect because of the systems that work against us.

My mission is this: to help you step into your power and attain your professional vision. I believe, with the right tools, strategies, and mindset, you can create the exact career, passion, salary and work/life balance you desire.

And it all starts with you.

Since you chose to carve out time in your busy schedule to pick up this book, chances are you are reflecting on the various experiences that impact your professional journey as an underrepresented professional. Over the course of your career, you have likely read countless books about professional advancement; attended career development workshops, trainings, and retreats; and followed self-proclaimed career "gurus" on social media. Perhaps you've found value in these educational endeavors—or perhaps, as you ingested these "best practices" and bits of advice, you've found yourself fighting anxiety, contending with imposter syndrome, or feeling defeated and undervalued. The inspirational quotes and high-level advice may have offered a momentary feeling of motivation and empowerment, but when you began to put those recommendations into action, you found yourself asking, "Why isn't this working for me?"

If this is your experience, you're not alone. As I discovered in my own journey, the tips, tricks, and fluffy professional advice floating around the business world won't reliably fast-track career success for people like us. In fact, the information I will present to you in this book will confirm what you already intuitively know: that your experience in the workplace *is* different from that of your white peers, and that what works for your colleagues will not always work for you. For example:

- It may not feel organic for you to highlight your successes and achievements during conversations with your managers, even if you are measurably outperforming your peers.
- You may not feel able to fully enjoy corporate perks like flexible paid time off or self-designed schedules for fear of how you may be perceived—even though some of your white colleagues maximize these benefits without a second thought, and with no repercussions.
- During performance reviews, you've found yourself blindsided by negative feedback you've never heard before, or get put on a performance plan (which can cost you your job) for things that earn your white counterparts nothing more than constructive feedback.

- You know you're worthy of the role, seniority, or salary you are trying to attain, but leadership has not bought into your value, and you keep getting sidelined while other, similarly qualified white peers are promoted.

For underrepresented professionals, the list goes on and on.

If any (or all) of the above sound familiar to you, I want you to know you're not alone. Some variation of the above has been the lived experience of every one of my underrepresented peers and leaders, and they are the lived experience of the thousands of professionals of color I work with today through Brij the Gap Consulting. When you accept the reality that the business landscape contains specific and unique challenges for people of color, toss out the pep talks and generic advice, and adopt proven strategies that will actually drive results in your career, you take your power back. By operating within the reality of how business *is,* right now, today, rather than how we wish it would or could be, we can begin to create real change and greater equity for all of us.

Beautiful opportunities are there for you. By implementing the strategies I will teach you in this book, you will save time and minimize frustration. You will take bigger leaps forward and fewer steps back. You will open avenues toward greater income, authority, and recognition. You will make empowering decisions, even if that means deciding to leave your company to another environment that serves you better. And, perhaps most importantly, you will pave the way for other underrepresented people to succeed in their chosen work as well.

If that feels exciting, urgent, and uncomfortable all at the same time, you're definitely in the right place. Growth is *supposed* to feel like that.

I wrote this book to share career advancement strategies that *actually work* for people like us. On these pages, you'll find the exact prescriptive strategies that I teach in my programs, and that have helped thousands of underrepresented professionals navigate the often-rough waters of professional advancement. This book is your playbook for attaining your current career goals today, and also adapting as your goals change throughout your journey. You can also decide which strategies and tools to modify so the approaches feel authentic and personalized to your specific career.

I've included several exercises in this book to help you take action and implement the strategies you will be learning. These are the same exercises I provide to my private clients and corporate groups. To help you complete these exercises with ease, I've created multiple worksheets and downloads for you, which you can access at www.devikabrij.com/thriveincolor. Just save a copy of each file to your Google Drive or hard drive, then work directly in the file.

While some of this work will focus on how to meet the challenges of implicit and explicit bias in corporate structures and leadership models, not all of it is externally focused. You will also be asked to recognize and shift self-defeating mindsets and behaviors that are holding you hostage and preventing you from reaching your vision. Because I care about your lasting success, I will speak to you bluntly and honestly, as if you were my client, my sister, my brother, or my best friend. I will challenge you with uncomfortable action steps while supporting you to adopt and implement powerful tools and tactics. You won't get empty motivational words from me; what I will teach you offers the *true* empowerment that comes from self-reliance. If you stick with me, I promise we will "Brij" the gap between where you are today and where you desire to be in your professional life.

I may never have the honor of meeting you face to face, but we are connected by our shared experiences. You are on time, and you are worthy of the success, acknowledgment, and abundance you desire. Your success matters to me, and to the world.

So, take a deep breath, and let's get to work.

Chapter One

STOP PLAYING IT SAFE

"**DEV, I CAN SEE** Chrissy gets along with you well. I think she could learn a lot from you about managing a large volume of client relationships and work. I trust you can help her succeed by working closely with her and acting as a mentor. Can you do that?"

I was an individual contributor in a sales and customer service role when my manager made that ask of me. Our division sold advertising products to customers who desired to market their products on our social media platform. I was working with our highest-revenue clients, including some of the largest companies in North America, and was responsible for helping our team meet quarterly and annual sales goals. I was great at my job and had wonderful relationships with my clients, who needed to be cultivated continually to ensure that our team met revenue quotas.

My manager had just hired Chrissy to our Account Management team, and she and I immediately connected. She was quiet and kept mostly to herself, but when she did engage, she was funny and kind. Although she was knowledgeable and qualified, the volume of work, pressure, and accountability was paralyzing for her. My manager took notice and tasked me with helping Chrissy become a better performer, even though Chrissy's position was more senior than mine.

This new mentorship role would add more work and hours to my already full plate, but I truly wanted Chrissy to feel successful on our team and in our company. And so, I agreed.

A few months later, it was time for company-wide performance reviews. My review was strong, and my manager had selected "meeting expectations" and "exceeding expectations" in all of the areas in which I was being measured. When it came time for me to discuss my career path and ask for feedback on how to make my advancement goals a reality within the company, the response was, "Just keep doing what you're doing. When an opportunity comes, you're in a great position to move up."

While I was relieved to know I was considered a high performer, I was deeply disappointed. Why was I the first person approached to help someone more senior than me do her job better, yet I wasn't being considered for promotions myself? It bothered me, but I kept telling myself, "Don't rock the boat. Someone else will gladly take your place."

And so, I smiled, thanked my manager for her time, and kept moving. I continued to work long hours, contribute to areas that fell outside the scope of the role I was hired to do, and drive success, all the while knowing I was valued but not invested in by decision-makers other than my direct manager.

While all of this was unfolding, my colleague and good friend, Sam, was facing a similar challenge to mine. He had a glowing reputation, everyone loved him, and he did great work. He had access to cool opportunities—like traveling to our various global offices to train new team members—but monetary and advancement incentives were not being offered.

When we met up to "spill the tea" on what was happening at work, Sam mentioned that he'd had a firm conversation with his manager about his promotion—or, more accurately, his lack thereof.

He said, "I basically told her, 'I've consistently proven that I'm operating above and beyond what's expected, and I need tangible next steps toward promotion, or I'll have to explore other opportunities.' I think she got the message."

I was proud of Sam. He's not the type that welcomes conflict, so I knew that couldn't have been an easy conversation for him. But mostly, I was ashamed of myself. Why was the thought of taking a similar stance so crippling for me? Why was I—a person often labeled a "firecracker"—so passive when it came to advocating for what I desired and deserved, even with leaders who I knew were in my corner?

At the time, this felt like a "me" problem. But over the years, I've discovered that this is very much a community problem. Underrepresented professionals are not only consistently offered unequal pay and passed over for growth opportunities—we consistently *accept* those things.

I loved my team, my clients, and my manager, but I was unwilling to stay in a role that felt like a dead end. Out of sheer frustration, I ended up taking a role in another organization within the company. That transition resulted in a $30,000 salary increase overnight.

Yes, you read that right. $30,000 in additional compensation. However, that role also came with immense stress and workplace trauma that changed my entire trajectory at a company I loved. (More on that later.)

Many times, I've wished I would have felt empowered to ask for what I *really* wanted, which was to grow my seniority and compensation on that original customer service and sales team. I felt like, by exiting while I was dissatisfied, I had let limitation, rather than opportunity and excitement, decide my career path. My transition got me a raise, but it didn't feel like a move made on my own terms. I also regretted leaving my incredibly united team, all women of color, who were each other's biggest champions. Our team's dynamic and culture was special. I was grateful to be a part of it but I also knew my career opportunities and compensation was limited unless I made a move.

WHO DECIDES WHAT YOU'RE WORTH?

- "Do what you have to do to be accepted."
- "Keep your head down and be the best performer."
- "Be grateful for what you have."
- "Keep your personal life and work separate."
- "Always be agreeable and easy to work with so you don't lose your job."
- "Don't ask for too much, because they can replace you with someone who wants what you have."
- "Dress and speak differently to fit in with your coworkers."

If you've received this well-meaning career advice from parents, aunties, uncles, friends, or mentors, you're not alone.

As underrepresented professionals, we have been conditioned to step back, pipe down, and fit in to stay safe. More, we have collectively hung onto ideologies and thoughts like these that were passed down across generations—despite their lack of accuracy and relevance in today's work environment.

Let's be clear: All of the above are simply variations on, "Play it safe." That is *not* good career advice—and it's even worse when we tell it to ourselves.

Although I felt like I was the only one getting those messages during my time in the corporate world, I know now that my experience is replicated across all industries for underrepresented professionals, regardless of the company they work for, their salary range, or how much seniority they have. Each time my clients share transparently around the challenges they face in the workplace, it feels like déjà vu. And while there have been advancements in corporate culture in recent years—since events in 2020 catalyzed a public reckoning around the history of racial injustice, corporations have been more vocal about their commitments to diversity, equity, and inclusion (DEI), and employee resource groups (ERGs) have expanded exponentially—the daily reality for many of us has barely changed. In fact, you may be wondering, "How much of this is real, and how much is for show?"

The impact of systemic racism in the workplace is real, and it isn't going to change overnight. I can attest, through my own work as a consultant to major organizations, that there are companies out there who truly believe in equity and are doing the work to understand these challenges and make positive changes, but racism and racial bias are complex problems with complex solutions, and the current paradigm will take time to unravel.

That's why it's vital that you, as an underrepresented professional, take control of your career and exercise the power you have over your own experience in the workplace. Whether you're in an entry-level position or an executive one, it's time to stop pretending that quiet diligence will get you where you want to go. It won't. Instead, it's time to claim your full potential and build a personal brand that will carry you forward into whatever future you desire.

So, take a moment to reflect on your career journey. Are you excited about where you're going? Do you feel like your hard work is actually moving you forward toward a concrete set of goals? Do you feel seen, heard, appreciated, and supported in your work environment? If the answers to these are "yes," I applaud you. You have created a powerful path for yourself. This book will help you refine that path and stay motivated as you continue to build.

But, if you're anything like I was, you might feel nervous, unprepared, underappreciated, discouraged, and unworthy. Frustration and overwhelm might feel like your new normal. Part of that is likely coming from an implicitly (or explicitly) racist culture within your company. But part of that feeling is coming from *you.*

I thought for a long time that it was up to others in the workplace to make me feel worthy, appreciated, and prepared. I didn't fully understand that it was also up to me to take a stand for my own value and educate the people around me about how I wanted and deserved to be received. Yes, in many ways I was being blocked in my desire for advancement—but I wasn't advocating for my advancement, either. I was still steeped in the generational ideologies that said, "Play it safe and don't ask for too much." I expected my managers to notice my hard work and elevate me beyond what I felt comfortable asking for on my own behalf—and when that didn't happen, I felt like it was a judgment on my worth. I was wrong.

Studies show that *60 percent* of career success hinges on our ability to advocate for ourselves. This is true across the board, including for underrepresented professionals. Therefore, it is our responsibility to learn to communicate our needs, our value, and our goals clearly and without hesitation across all professional settings—and the best way to do that is to build a strong professional brand that backs up the fact that you deserve what you're asking for. The strategies you'll learn in this book will support you in doing exactly that.

PUT YOURSELF FIRST

I'm not here to tell you that you *need* to change how you're approaching your career.

However, I can attest—both from my own experience and those of the thousands of underrepresented individuals I've advised and taught over the years—that if you don't learn to put yourself first at work, you can and will lose the peace, confidence, time, money, and opportunities that you've been craving. In the situation I shared above, and in many more before and since, that was exactly what happened for me.

Putting yourself first at work isn't about making selfish power plays, dominating every conversation, or stoking an unhealthy level of ego. Rather, it's about creating space to gain clarity around your strengths and goals, giving yourself opportunities to gain confidence, and continually implementing key strategies to fuel your momentum. When you know how to support yourself to bridge the gap between where you are and where you want to be, you will break the cycle that, in my work, I call the "3D Cycle of Frustration"—a cycle in which many of us have been trapped for too long.

In this case, "3D" stands for Discontentment, Defeat, and Doubt. These emotions regularly emerge for individuals when they approach professional advancement without strategy. When you are in the "Gap"—that obscure place between your comfort zone or current situation and the "something greater" you feel called toward—it's easy to get sucked into that 3D Cycle without realizing it.

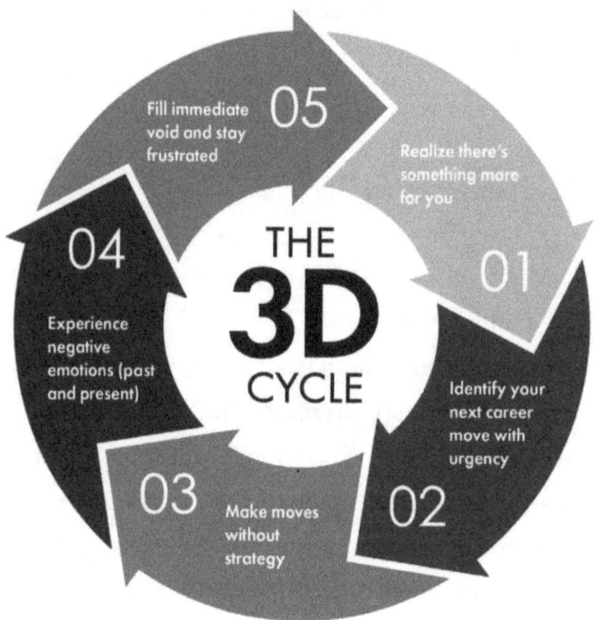

For most people I work with, the 3D Cycle looks like this:

1). You feel that you need or want something more from your career than you are currently experiencing.

2). You identify your next career desire with urgency.

3). Excited to create a change, you make career moves without proper direction, strategy, and support.

4). Negative emotions from the past and present emerge (like feeling undervalued, unwanted, frustrated with the process, dissatisfied with timelines, etc.)

5). You fill the void by taking a less than ideal role, settling for less than your desired salary, or taking the only option being presented just to end the cycle of discontentment, defeat, and doubt.

Within a short time, the opportunity you seized while operating in urgency feels all wrong—which leads you to start the whole cycle again.

My dissatisfaction around what was happening with Chrissy and my reviews led me to jump the gun with a transition that wasn't fully aligned with my goals. I didn't want to leave the department. Our team consisted entirely of women of color and we all supported and championed one another. My manager truly cared about my success, and I enjoyed the work I was doing. But I wanted to be valued and rewarded beyond our team for my contributions. I don't know whether that would or could have happened if I'd stayed and created a solid plan for advancement—but I do *know* that my knee-jerk move, even with the huge bump in pay, was not the right choice either.

Despite what you may currently feel, the ownership of your career is yours. Therefore, it's vital to remember that your career decisions should be made from a place of putting yourself first. The way to break the 3D Cycle isn't to constantly move from role to role, or from company to company. Instead, taking the time to properly reflect, evaluate options, and present solutions can be a game-changer—not only for your results, but for your overall wellness.

WHAT'S YOURS AND WHAT ISN'T

There is a widespread belief among underrepresented professionals that decision-makers have more impact and influence on our careers than we do ourselves.

Yes, there are many factors at work that are out of your control—but you also have more power than you realize. In fact, it was this exact realization that catapulted me into my greatest career moves and successes. Some things aren't up to me—but many things are, and I can choose to exercise my power in those areas.

The reality is, there are two distinct sets of responsibilities: one that your company should own, and the other that you own.

It's your company's responsibility to foster a work environment that is inclusive and where all employees can bring their best selves to work, be supported and nurtured through learning and development, treated fairly, and have an equal shot at success. If your company isn't doing this—or at least genuinely working toward it, because let's face it, we have a long way to go—they are not doing their part, and you can use that information to make informed decisions about your next steps.

Your responsibility, on the other hand, is to produce quality work, build positive relationships with decision-makers, understand and communicate your development needs, and evaluate and determine options for your own career progression. More, it's your job to create and scale your professional brand and become an advocate for your values, accomplishments, and needs.

If both parties are fulfilling their responsibilities, you can come to the negotiating table with confidence that everyone is invested in the best outcome.

Many of the personal responsibilities listed above will not feel organic to you. In fact, they can feel exhausting, "extra," or like you're brown-nosing. They most certainly won't feel like "playing it safe."

I hear you. I once felt the same. I've gotten the job. I've not gotten the job. I've been promoted. I've been terminated. I've successfully negotiated great compensation packages. I've under-negotiated and learned that my peers were making significantly more than me. I've had incredible successes and epic failures. In these ways, you and I aren't really that different.

However, as a former individual contributor, people leader, and now consultant to major organizations and professionals across all demographics, industries, and seniorities, I can tell you that claiming and acting on these responsibilities is *the most accurate predictor of success* for underrepresented professionals.

The Power of Self-Governance

In working with underrepresented peers, clients, and partners over the years, I've noticed that most people tend to hold one of two specific mindsets when approaching career advancement in their workplaces: "problem" mindset and "possibility" mindset.

The first group, those with a "problem" mindset, lead with the belief that, "It's always going to be like this, and it's never going to change." This belief is often rooted in anger and disappointment from seeing the horrendous cycles of racism, bigotry, and systemic oppression that have created, and continue to create, barriers, challenges, and heartache for people of color. Common thoughts problem thinkers have include: "I could never do that," "It's never going to work out for me," "I'll never get what I deserve," and "It's impossible." The instant reaction for this group of people is to put their guard up. Even if someone presents a solution, problem thinkers tend to point out the one negative within that solution. When this mindset is present, any steps toward advancement can feel harder than necessary, or even futile.

The second group, possibility thinkers, lead with the belief that, "There must be some other way!" as they continuously pursue career advancement. If they can't go through the front door, they'll strategize ways to go through the back door or even through the window. They understand that, despite the unfair systems and environments they are working within, they can choose to show up consistently, do the best they can, and operate in a way they are proud of. They choose not to submerge themselves in situations they cannot control. That is the expectation and responsibility they have for themselves.

We all have a right to our experience. We all have a right to our anger. We all have a right to feel how we feel. And, at the same time, we need to know where to go from here, and what we actually want for ourselves in our lives and careers. There is no single solution to this massive problem. We have to build many, many bridges until the gap is closed.

By picking up this book, and by doing the work I'm outlining on these pages, you are bridging the gap.

What I'm presenting to you in this book is the first step toward a bigger vision. Creating and refining your personal brand as an underrepresented professional is not the only step, but it is one of the most important because it will set you on a proactive path.

So, right here, right now, I want you to imagine a bridge in your mind. The starting point is where you are standing in this moment. The end point is where you accomplish your current career goal or desire.

In a perfect world, we would all step onto this bridge confidently and take bold, proactive leaps until we reached our destination. Our leaders and decision-makers would meet us in the middle and walk toward the finish line with us, extending their hands to guide us to our ultimate destination and goal.

Could that be realistic? Absolutely. Could your workplaces, decision-makers, and leaders be willing to do the work necessary on their parts to create a safe environment where you are consistently understood, supported, and encouraged to thrive? Yes. In fact, many of them already are willing. However, most of us are not experiencing that reality now.

If leaders meeting you in the middle of that bridge is not something you can expect at this time, you have three choices:

1). Be angry, exhausted, discouraged, and demotivated by the systemic challenges that continue to disadvantage people of color and keep us from stepping on that bridge at all. (If this is where you are, it's okay. It's valid to be present in these feelings.)

2). Set aside the frustration, anger, and disappointment, and take just two steps onto that bridge. This approach opens you to learning how to take more intentional leaps and become more empowered despite the circumstances which remain out of your control.

3). Continue placing one foot in front of the other so you can work your way across the bridge one intentional step at a time. The bridge will be shaky, the wind will blow, and support may not be offered, yet you continue to make those purpose-driven steps with the intention of crossing over to the other side.

Wherever you are is valid. Each approach is valid. However, when you are tired of being angry and are ready to accept that, although systemic racism and other issues will not change overnight, there are things you can do to improve your own circumstances and experience, you will feel called toward steps two and three. You don't have to give in to the challenges you face; you can move through them, over them, or around them! There is room for great growth even in limiting environments—and the self-respect you will gain by taking control of your personal bridge will be worth all the effort you put in. When you practice self-governance and take responsibility only for what's yours, no one can dim your light. You can thrive in full color.

***

As you've probably guessed by now, this book is not dedicated to solving systemic issues or even issues of racism and discrimination within corporations. That is a different conversation, and even the most dedicated DEI professionals cannot solve such problems immediately or without the cooperation of many individuals. Instead, this book will focus on the most immediate and powerful changes within your power to make as an individual—changes you can start making right now that will actually move the needle for you in your individual career. We can't change others, but we can most certainly change ourselves.

If you're feeling overwhelmed, I get it—but fear not. This book will help you identify the prescriptive steps to transform your mind, your energy, and your professional path so you can begin taking full ownership of your success.

My goal is not to give you a running list of tasks that feel impossible to achieve. The last thing I want you to do is reinvent the wheel or add more to-do's to your already full plate! Rather, what you'll learn in this book will teach you to make key personal responsibilities part of your natural day-to-day routine, so you can expand on and replicate them in each new season of your career. I'll share attainable and realistic goals and strategies to help you start taking action today and stop feeling like you have to sacrifice what you truly desire because the world isn't fully on your side.

Because in the end, our success isn't only for us. It's for every person who looks like us who is coming up behind us. By taking responsibility for our professional success, we will make it easier for others like us to get there as well.

Chapter Two

PERFORMING UNDER THE MICROSCOPE

WHILE I WAS WORKING for a large social networking company, I traveled frequently for meetings. It was one of my favorite parts of the job.

The company had an internal travel booking program with preselected hotel options. We were encouraged to use these hotels because they offered discounted rates for company employees.

I'm the type of person who will keep going back to the same hotels, restaurants, and stores that offer me a pleasant experience. Plus, who has time to research hotels when you're on the road all the time? So, when I found a hotel on the company's "preferred" list that was comfortable, safe, and in an area of Midtown that put us within walking distance of the office, it naturally became a habit to stay there every time I and my team went to New York.

Four years into my tenure with this company, I switched departments, and my trips to New York became more frequent.

A few months into the role, a new manager, whom I'll call Heather, was hired. Heather and I had met a year prior to me switching teams and her becoming my manager, and I was excited when I learned we'd be working together. She seemed nice and she had this kind of sarcastic, cool energy. She was always poking fun at people on our team, mostly the guys, and loved hosting team events at her house where she'd set up beer pong, flip cup, and other drinking games. She very much wanted to be the "chill leader" on a performance-driven team where there was a high demand to drive revenue within our sales roles. She was nice to me, but I immediately felt the difference in my relationship with her compared to my peers. As the only woman of color on the team, there were moments where I thought I might be overthinking the way her interactions with me seemed forced and awkward—and then, I'd observe how much more relaxed and organic her behavior was with everyone else.

Turns out, I wasn't overthinking at all. Things quickly grew uncomfortable

I had scheduled a trip to New York for a client meeting two weeks prior, choosing the same flight and hotel options as I always had in my previous department. The booking confirmations were automatically sent to Heather's email, as they had also been sent to my previous manager. Heather and I had several conversations leading up to the trip, and my travel plans were never commented upon.

However, when I returned from New York, a calendar invite popped up in my inbox. "Heather and Devika Connect," it read. It was scheduled for the following day, which insinuated urgency, but I didn't think much of it. *She probably wants to talk about the client account,* I thought.

When I signed into our virtual meeting, I was greeted with the usual pleasantries: "How are you? How was New York? Tell me about the meeting with the client." Then, the conversation took a turn.

"I want to talk to you about your choice of hotel," Heather said. "I was completely shocked to see that you booked such an expensive hotel when there are plenty of other options to choose from in the vicinity."

I felt my face get hot. I felt embarrassed, but I didn't know why. "That's where I've stayed for the past four and a half years. It's on the approved list on our booking platform."

"No, it's not."

Truly shocked, I stammered, "It isn't? I'm sorry. Maybe it was removed at some point? I've always stayed there, every time I've been to New York."

I went into "explain myself" mode—not even pausing to reflect on why I even *needed* to explain myself. I knew that several of my colleagues across various departments also stayed at that hotel.

"I had no idea that this would be a problem," I concluded.

"You're not acting like an owner, Devika," Heather said. "I'm not telling you to stay at a Motel 6 or something, but this is excessive."

"I'll keep that in mind in future." I just wanted to get off of this call. It was becoming more awkward by the minute.

Heather went on. "Would you stay at this hotel if you weren't traveling for work?"

She was clearly insinuating that I wouldn't spend my own money to stay at a nice hotel. "Yes, I have," I replied. "A few times."

"Well, the rate for this is over three times our company approved rate per night."

I was further confused by that comment. "I've never been given a preferred per-night rate as a guideline. What is that rate?"

"You don't need to get all defensive. I'm just calling out an area I need for you to be mindful of. It looks like taking feedback from your manager is something you'll need to work on."

My stomach was in my throat at this point. I couldn't defend myself or ask for more clarity without Heather thinking I was being rude and unable to take feedback. So, I simply said, "Okay, I'm sorry again."

I thought that would be the last of it. But our conversation was quickly followed up by an email.

> *"Thank you for speaking with me today about my concerns regarding your performance. I have concerns around some behaviors that are not in line with our culture and values. You booked a hotel at three times the company's preferred rate. When in doubt on an internal policy, check with me to clarify. We will continue to work together and monitor progress in our reoccurring one-to-ones."*

An honest error around a hotel booking—if it even *was* an error, which I honestly wasn't sure of at this point—was now being positioned as bad performance and lack of integrity.

I was mind-blown. Any ounce of trust I'd had in Heather went out the window in that moment. She was clearly making a record of my "problematic behavior" by recapping our conversation in a follow-up email.

Obviously, the professional brand and trust I'd built within my former department hadn't translated with this move. But I knew this game—and I played it right back.

I responded to the email restating that I was not aware that the hotel had been removed from the preferred list, and that, unless I started a new search every time I booked a trip (which would not be an effective use of company time), there was no way I could have known. I committed to finding a new hotel for my next trip, and asked for clarification on the rate Heather kept referring to as well as any other rates and policies I might not be aware of so I could make appropriate choices in future. I closed the email with what seemed like my twentieth apology. It was important for me to respond with the facts instead of letting Heather frame the situation as if I was being intentionally shady.

Heather didn't like that approach. In the twenty-four hours it took her to respond to my email, she called the travel company to see if the hotel had ever been included on the company approved list. She wanted to catch me in a lie. She needed to be right in this situation.

> *"Devika. This is the second conversation we've had about hotel choice. We have discussed guidance on booking travel. We do not, and will not, provide a dollar amount for you to stay within. It is too difficult to monitor the change in travel costs by location or season. Instead, my guidance is and has always been, to act like an owner. When there are multiple hotel options available to you in the travel booking tool and one hotel is a lower amount and you book the higher amount hotel that is not acting like an owner. You should evaluate your options and use sound judgment to determine what hotel makes most sense. If I have to babysit your decisions, it's not going to work."*

This was getting uncomfortable and, quite frankly, confusing. My hands were bound. I could try to prove that I am, in fact, a person of integrity and sound judgment, and press harder on the hotel rate that seemed to exist in one conversation and not in the next—all the while knowing that Heather was labeling me as "defensive" and deflecting blame—or, I could try to salvage my now-very-awkward relationship with my manager who had already indirectly threatened my employment with that "it's not going to work" statement, accept ownership of the change that needed to be made around the hotel bookings, and shut my mouth.

I chose the latter.

Days later, I was still upset and embarrassed by the encounter. It didn't sit well with me that my integrity was being questioned. I also wondered why I was getting called out for staying at this particular hotel when several of my colleagues were still staying there regularly.

I pulled my former manager aside and asked for her advice on what to do. She and I had stayed at that exact hotel several times when we traveled together when I was on her team. She replied, "I shouldn't be saying this Devi, but Heather called me the other day and asked me if you had demonstrated these behaviors while you were on my team. I told her no, and explained that you would never take advantage of work policies. Clearly, this is something she is concerned about. I encourage you to continue seeking clarity and include her so she sees that you are being mindful of whatever it is that she's worried about. I know it sucks to be questioned, but you have a great brand at this company, and I want you to be protected."

It was well-meaning advice. But this approach didn't help my relationship with Heather. She'd made up her mind about me, and that prevented her from hearing me in situations that could have been easily resolved if she had been willing to listen.

Heather's constant need to correct me regarding something I was doing that made her "uncomfortable" became too regular. Multiple times a week, she sent emails questioning me. There were random "check-ins" to make sure I was working well with my team (insinuating something was wrong that I was unaware of). She also called me out for working from home too often, even though my white peers were only in the office once or twice a week. Thinking back to my previous manager's advice, I ignored many more similar situations—but eventually, Heather's blatant bias and unfair treatment pushed me out of the company. (I'll share that story later in the book.)

YOU ARE NOT ALONE

Research from the National Bureau of Economic Research (NBER) shows that ethnically diverse workers are scrutinized more than their white counterparts, resulting in employment durations being lower.* So, if you feel as though you are constantly under a microscope at work ... well, you're probably right.

Recently, I was coaching a client, Bri, on a challenge similar to the one I'd faced years before with Heather. Bri and I had worked together a year prior around her transition from contractor to full-time employee at a globally recognized company. Bri got the job, doubled her salary, and was thrilled about the work she was doing. However, in the year since that transition occurred, things had changed dramatically.

"Devika, I need to get out of this company *fast*."

**C. Cavounidis, K. Lang. "NBER Working Paper Series: Discriminatino and Worker Evaluation." October 2015; JEL No. J71*

I was instantly concerned. "Bri, you were thrilled about this company a year ago. What changed?"

Bri went on to explain a series of events where she was reprimanded for situations that were either misunderstandings or totally not her fault. One example she shared included a time when her manager asked her to post a report on the company-wide news feed where employees shared insights with one another. Bri let her manager know that she didn't feel the report was polished enough to post on a public forum. Her manager advised her to continue revising the report and share it when she felt more comfortable. Unfortunately, Bri heard, "Post it *if* you feel comfortable," which made the ask from her manager sound optional. When she ultimately chose not to post the report, her manager questioned Bri's desire to work for the company.

"If you don't want to be here," the manager told her, "there are many others who do."

If her manager had allowed Bri to provide context on the miscommunication and how it happened, her manager might have understood the oversight.

"Did you take responsibility for your part in this event?" I asked.

"I did, and I apologized repeatedly. But in my manager's mind, I disobeyed her and now she thinks I don't care about working here."

Bri's manager went down the same path as Heather did with me. A seemingly trivial situation would begin a sequence of being negatively called out, compared to other team members who were manager favorites, slapped with disciplinary action for things that white employees would never be called out for—and ultimately having her employment threatened.

The unfairness and tension of the situation led Bri to work in constant fear and anxiety, which caused her to make mistakes she would never have made otherwise. Unfortunately, these mistakes landed her on a performance plan.

It saddened me that a talented, smart, and dedicated employee like Bri could go from having a strong professional brand across her team to being on a performance plan and her employment threatened in the space of less than a year. Hearing her story brought back my own workplace trauma. And, at the same time, I was glad for my experience with Heather, because it led me to learn strategies to navigate these complex situations which I now share with my underrepresented professional clients.

"Here's what I wish I knew when I was dealing with my old manager," I told Bri. "First, immediately stop apologizing as your initial response. Apologizing profusely for simple miscommunications and mistakes shows leaders that you are at their mercy—that they are right, you are wrong, and that you deserve whatever consequences they decide to impose. Instead, ask clarifying questions, acknowledge your part in the mistake, and clearly communicate what you will do differently next time. Then, ask for help in areas where you need to operate more effectively. This shifts the balance from 'I'm wrong, you're right,' to you taking accountability only for your part in the situation. Then, follow up with a recap of what was discussed to make sure your account and your manager's are always aligned. This way, she can't surprise you with negative feedback in performance reviews or in conversations with HR."

Bri and I worked on how she could implement all of the above, and she got to work. There were definitely situations where she was uncomfortable speaking up—where her voice and hands would shake, and where she had to bite her cheek to stop herself from apologizing just so it would all go away. But the more she stood her ground, asked clarifying questions, and tracked her interactions, the more confident she became. She went from feeling anxiety-ridden every day to standing her ground with peers and decision-makers. She was determined not to allow anyone to make her doubt herself and her qualifications.

Over time, the attacks became less and less frequent, but ultimately the trust lost with her leader caused Bri to seek a position with another company where she was able to negotiate a superior compensation package. She now works with a leader who acknowledges her contributions and pushes her to develop her skills. She finally feels like she's found a place to belong and thrive.

Reading this story, you may think, "You make it sound so simple—but it's not."

You're right. I didn't feel equipped to do any of the above when I was working with Heather, and Bri didn't feel equipped to stand her ground despite having proof of her contributions. We both needed to develop a whole range of skills to feel confident enough to stand our ground with employers and managers, take responsibility for only what was ours, and refuse to apologize for situations and events that weren't our fault.

Communicating in a way that supported and expanded my professional brand took practice, and it wasn't always easy. I made lots of mistakes. But, in the end, it made a huge difference in how I was perceived, treated, and communicated with in my career.

GET IN THE DRIVER'S SEAT

I know I don't need to expound further on the unfair treatment underrepresented professionals face at companies both large and small. The challenges we encounter are multidimensional—and there are no easy answers.

On one hand, bias and unintentional (or worse, intentional) discrimination within the company and its leadership create painful and deflating experiences for underrepresented employees. People of color face unfair treatment inside and outside of work every day. Most of us have become almost immune to, or expectant of, these situations. The gaslighting that occurs when we try to problem-solve with people who lead with intentional or unintentional bias shuts us down. It's simply too exhausting to feel blamed, unworthy, and unprepared all the time, or to constantly fight to change the perceptions of others. So, we accept the bias as a part of our reality and endure it job after job, position after position, manager after manager, until we finally get fed up and leave the company (or get pushed out)—only to start the same cycle in our next role.

On the other hand, how an individual does or does not step up and own their personal brand, self-advocate, ask the right questions, and communicate in a manner that protects their reputation and work is also a factor. Like Bri did so powerfully in her own role, you can change the outcome of a situation by changing how you contribute to it.

I know you're tired. I know you're frustrated from feeling like you have to do the absolute *most* in every situation to receive opportunities that your counterparts receive proactively. I continue to see deflating and unfair experiences happen over and over again with the underrepresented professionals I work with today.

But I want you to ask yourself honestly, "What will happen if I continue this cycle?"

I submit for your consideration one of my favorite quotes from the great Michelle Obama: "When they go low, we go high." I'm not asking you to "go higher" by absolving decision-makers of accountability or stoically enduring unfair treatment. I'm asking you to create the highest version of yourself by continuously operating from a posture that drives your success and thereby creating a different and more enjoyable experience for yourself and those who will come after you.

The strategies in this book will set you up to handle situations like the ones I've described differently and with greater clarity and confidence. The strategy of showing up as an advocate for yourself and your professionalism is multilayered and will require you to make some key changes in your mindset, approach, and responses—but, ultimately, it all distills down to this: own your part of the equation, so that no matter what unfolds, you know that you have done your best for yourself, your values, and your vision for your career.

So, it's time to get into the driver's seat.

I want you to imagine you are in the passenger's seat of a vehicle being driven by someone else. Take a long, deep breath in. Envision all the ideologies, damaging experiences, and toxic leaders you've encountered in your career up until this point as junk piled up inside the car. Now, release your breath while simultaneously tossing all of those thoughts, experiences, and people out the car window—and out of your mind.

Then, imagine yourself getting out of the vehicle and taking over the driver's seat.

That's where you are now: in the driver's seat, owning the direction and pace of your career goals and desires.

Let's move forward.

Chapter Three

THE SELF-ADVOCACY DILEMMA

ANDRE, A FORMER colleague from my tech days, experienced workplace trauma that affected his professional journey for several years. Working under a perfectionist, difficult-to-please leader who was quick to point out every mistake and slow to acknowledge success delivered a heavy blow to Andre's self-esteem. He was fully committed to his work and the company, and had a solid performance record, but because he never felt like an asset to his team, he rarely raised his hand for promotion opportunities—even those for which he would be a great fit.

A few years into his role, a rare opportunity to become a people manager came up. Knowing this job opening would not come again for a long time, Andre decided to alert his manager to his intention to apply. His manager instantly responded, "I'm not sure you are ready for a manger position, Andre." No reasons, no discussion, just instant rejection.

Although his confidence was shattered, Andre took the rejection gracefully. A few months later, he decided to leave the company for a role at another reputable tech company. Yet, he carried his disappointment and rejection with him. When an opportunity to put his name in the hat for a promotion or opportunity to advance came up, Andre didn't bother. He knew he was a strong performer and had a great relationship with his new manager, but the chance of being unvalued and rejected again was too scary.

When a second opportunity to apply for a more senior position came up, Andre ignored it and encouraged his peers to apply. His manager read Andre's lack of action as a lack of desire for the role. Andre's peer ended up receiving the role, resulting in a $40,000 salary bump.

Shortly after this, during the company-wide performance review cycle, Andre approached his manager for a pay increase after two consistent years of exceptional performance.

His manager asked, "I'm curious. Why didn't you apply for the manager role? I would have loved to endorse you."

"I wasn't sure if I was ready," Andre answered.

His manager went on to explain that Andre was more prepared and equipped than he gave himself credit for, and encouraged him to voice his desire for any opportunity. She then proceeded to give Andre a 3 percent pay increase. Although Andre was thankful for the raise and his manager's vote of confidence, he couldn't help but think of the additional compensation he'd left on the table by not going for the manager role. He was angry at himself for letting the rejection and trauma of his past workplace dictate his current experience and readiness.

That series of events prompted Andre to begin to explore with a therapist why he didn't feel worthy or able to take on higher-visibility roles. Through acknowledging his habits, stepping into vulnerability, and receiving support from his therapist, Andre was able to identify situations of rejection both in his personal and professional life, including his relationship with his manager in the former company, which deeply affected his confidence and abilities.

Andre began to advocate for himself as part of this process of self-healing. He taped a Post-it on his bathroom mirror with "$40,000" written on it to remind himself what he'd lost when he was operating from fear of rejection and lack of confidence.

Today, six years after leaving his previous toxic workplace, Andre is the VP of Digital Ad Sales at one of the largest fashion companies in the world, as well as the executive sponsor for their Black Inclusion Group, where he mentors Black employees on how to effectively advocate for and negotiate their needs. He is an amazing success story, and I am absolutely thrilled for him—both as a friend and as a fellow professional of color. Watching him own his worth in his career is truly inspirational.

WHAT'S YOUR CONTRIBUTION WORTH?

As an underrepresented professional, one or more of the following statements are likely true for you:

- You're ready for advancement—a new role, transitioning industries or departments, a promotion, a salary increase, or moving from an individual contributor role to a people manager role (or a more senior role in general)—but are uncertain whether the career path you desire will be open to you.

- You have trouble communicating your value or making asks during performance review cycles, self-assessments, general career conversations, internal interviews, meetings with senior leaders, or one-to-one meetings with your manager.

- You desire to secure and build authentic relationships with mentors, sponsors, and other leaders who have decision-making power within your organization, but aren't sure how to ask.

- You understand the importance of having a professional brand, but you are unclear on how to create your own and how to get others to adopt it within your company, team, and industry.

If you're reading this and thinking, "Wow, I am *not* good at advocating for myself," you're not alone. After working with thousands of underrepresented professionals at some of the most notable companies in the world, I can confirm that most of us struggle with self-advocacy—and often with good reason.

As we've explored in the previous chapters, workplace trauma, biases, and limitations are everywhere for underrepresented professionals. While each of us experiences these things to different degrees and in different ways, I think it's safe to say that all of us have weathered challenges that have impacted, and may continue to impact, the way we show up in our professional journey. These things are not okay and need to be addressed and changed.

However, there's also the question of what we bring to the table.

What is it costing us, individually and collectively, to not address our own inhibitors to self-advocacy? What is it costing us, in both compensation and time, to allow the abuse, ignorance, bias, and lack of support to infiltrate and diminish our view of ourselves? What is it costing us, and those who will come after us, to avoid the necessary internal changes that will allow us to come to the bargaining table with full faith in ourselves and our contributions?

Now is the time to take proactive and intentional steps toward getting what you want and deserve in your career. The frameworks I will share in Part II of this book will give you a powerful foundation for growth. However, none of those frameworks will be effective for you unless you are willing, able, and committed to self-advocacy.

Self-advocacy is the overarching solution to career development and advancement. It is the ability to speak up for yourself, communicate your needs, and express your feedback—including but not limited to sharing your accomplishments, asking for a raise or promotion, requesting to be added or removed from a project, asking for resources to become a better professional, and sharing feedback about your company, team, and clients.

Self-advocacy is not a tactic or script. It's a consistent mindset and belief that your needs and ideas are important, and that you will give yourself permission to pursue them. It's also a skill that supports self-awareness, independence, and self-confidence.

The key to effective self-advocacy is keeping an open mind and remembering that nothing is written in stone. You have the power to make a case for yourself, open up a dialogue, and pivot when necessary to make you feel most successful.

Developing a self-advocating mindset will be *the most critical thing you will do* in your career.

Here are some examples of what self-advocacy can look like:

- Asking for incentives like development opportunities or higher pay.
- Asking for help or resources for yourself (education, coaching, introductions to mentors, sponsors, etc.).
- Applying for a promotion or shifting to another department within the company.
- Making requests for the team that you manage.
- Communicating ideas or feedback to drive the company and your team forward.
- Raising your hand for a project.
- Asking to be removed from a project that isn't a good fit for you.
- Expressing your work/life balance needs.

Most professionals of color only speak up for themselves and share their accomplishments and professional value in-depth once or twice a year during company-mandated performance reviews. Sure, you may sprinkle in a few examples of what you're proud about in your conversations with your managers, but real self-advocacy means being consistent both in how you share information and how regularly you do so to drive impact in your career. Performance review cycles and self-assessments are actually the worst times to talk about your accomplishments because your manager is focused on putting together several performance reviews for their direct reports in addition to their own self-assessment that is due to their managers. Even concrete examples of how you're driving success for the company, your team, your cross-functional colleagues, and your clients are likely to get lost in the shuffle during those periods. (Not to mention, all of your peers and colleagues are actively sharing their own accomplishments during that time, which will make everyone's shares less memorable.) However, if you have multiple touch points about your career achievements, development, and advancement goals throughout the year, your performance review will feel more like the icing on the cake.

The Numbers Don't Lie

Without effective self-advocacy, career progression and advancement will be a slow climb up a very steep hill.

As I mentioned in Chapter One, 60 percent of your success hinges on your ability to advocate for yourself. However, I'll bet that you've assumed, as I used to, that performance is still a major driver in your career advancement.

You'd be wrong. Performance only accounts for *10 percent* of your career success.

Why is this true? There are a few reasons.

First, strong performance is an expectation of all employees, regardless of industry or seniority. Those who don't meet expectations for the role they were hired to do cannot expect rewards. Being great at your job is a bare minimum requirement and is why you were selected over other candidates for your position.

The truth is, most professionals are meeting the expectations of their roles, even if their performance is not as good as others on their team. This is why it's so frustrating when someone with mediocre performance elevates their work boldly to management and, as a result, gains access that better performers should have been selected for. Given the statistic I shared above, we can see that these gains happen not as a result of strong performance, but rather as a result of strong self-advocacy. Such individuals have mastered the art of driving exposure to their achievements and value. They know how to position themselves to decision-makers as the right person at the right time.

Of course, being a strong performer is a necessary foundation for becoming a great self-advocate. You need to be able to stand on your own record with confidence. Moreover, you cannot expect leaders to reward you with advancement opportunities when you are not successfully meeting the expectations of your current role and responsibilities. However, self-advocacy has a role to play even if you are struggling: if you are not performing to expectations, you can advocate for the support and resources you need to overcome challenges, get up to speed, or even change your role or department. The reality is, we will all struggle in our careers at some point in time—and those times are when we will need our self-advocacy skills the most. It's not realistic to expect that you will always be the perfect top performer. Challenges in your personal life, obstacles outside of your control, and many other factors can lead to diminished performance. Depending on how you navigate through these situations, you may be able to minimize corrective actions like a performance improvement plan (which may sometimes lead to termination) and instead turn your challenges into stepping stones to even greater success.

So, if 60 percent of your career success stems from your ability to self-advocate and create exposure around your contributions and achievements, and just 10 percent results from your actual performance, what makes up the remaining 30 percent?

That comes from your *reputation*—aka, your personal brand.

How your leaders, managers, colleagues, mentors, sponsors, and clients perceive you is a huge driver in your upward mobility. Without a strong reputation across your team and organization, it can be more challenging for your managers to advance and reward you. For example, if you are interviewing for a Team Lead role, but your reputation today displays that you tend to be a complainer and are resistant to helping your colleagues, it will be clear to decision-makers that you do not have the reputation or characteristics to be successful in this role. This is why developing and scaling a strong and authentic professional brand is imperative to your success. You must first develop a strong professional brand before you can effectively self-advocate.

We will learn to do this together in Part II of this book.

BARRIERS TO SELF-ADVOCACY

Aside from bias and exclusion, which are easy to recognize, below are some common but less obvious barriers to self-advocacy that can interfere with building your personal brand and achieving career success.

Upbringing and Culture

We've touched on this in previous chapters, but it's worth revisiting here. No matter how hard we try, we cannot separate who we are as individuals from who we are as professionals. Where you come from and what you have experienced will always influence who you are.

However, while our families, cultures, and faith practices absolutely instill positive qualities and characteristics that elevate us in the workplace, they can also inhibit our career journeys. Common threads of playing it safe, always being grateful, and not drawing attention to ourselves are common for many, if not most, of the underrepresented professionals I've worked with. Humility is ingrained into our actions—and it's reinforced by our families and social groups. If you mention wanting to approach a pay increase conversation or apply for a role that will give you better growth opportunities, you may be met with responses like, "Be grateful you work for that company!" "So many people would do anything to be in your position!" While I absolutely agree with practicing gratitude and humility, I recognize that leading with humility has inhibited the majority of ethnically diverse individuals to ask for what they deserve and strive for more. You should not feel guilty—or be expected to feel guilty—for asking for what you know you are capable of having. Gratitude for what you have now and excitement for what's to come can exist simultaneously.

Another key theme in upbringing for culturally and ethnically diverse individuals includes "perform the best." Many parents who belong to ethnic groups place a high value on grades and performance in school, due to the expectation that performance always leads to rewards. Almost every single professional I have worked with has adopted the concept that, if they simply perform better than everyone else, rewards and promotions will organically occur. Knowing that performance equates to only 10 percent of career success, it's easy to see that this mentality is not only unhelpful but limiting.

Lastly, did you grow up hearing, "Keep your personal life at home?" I did. Often, ethnically diverse individuals, especially first- and second-generation immigrants, fear being vocal about what matters to them, what they need to make time for, and their boundaries overall. They fear how this may impact how they are perceived at work. For example, I once managed a mother of two small kids who would mention that she needed to leave the office at 3:00 p.m. some days, but never really did so. When I asked her about it, she said that she wanted to pick up her children from daycare, but due to workload backlog she often called her babysitter to pick them up instead. It was now clear to me why she appeared so much more frustrated at the end of the day: she felt like she was letting her children down for the sake of keeping up with her workload. Her father, an immigrant from the Philippines, often told her that leaving work early to be present for her children would jeopardize her career. Although it was done in love, his tendency to inflict concerns from his own experiences was not helping her. Thankfully, I was able to convince her that family came first and that her desire to pick up her children from daycare had no effect on how I viewed her commitment. She breathed an audible sigh of relief. Soon, she started leaving the office early to pick up her children but would often sign on later in the afternoon to make up for lost time. She was more productive and motivated than ever knowing that her colleagues understood what was important to her personally, as well as professionally.

Stereotypes

Fear of stereotypes is also a major cause of self-advocacy dilemmas for underrepresented professionals. Many of us have experienced stereotyping at some point in our lives, whether in a personal or professional context. In effort to avoid these unfair, untrue, and disrespectful judgments, underrepresented professionals may code-switch by changing their mannerisms, way of speaking, appearance, and other factors to conform to the expectations of corporate culture (which has been generally and systemically white).

A short list of common stereotypes in the workplace includes, "Angry Black Woman," "Fiery Latina," and "Quiet Asian." In an effort to not be stereotyped, a Black woman in the workplace may intentionally withhold her point of view to avoid being perceived as angry. A Hispanic individual may contain their emotions when responding to feedback to avoid being perceived as overly excitable. An Asian individual may go out of their way to be perceived as a social and extroverted leader, even if it does not feel organic to their personality style.

To an extent, I believe that *all* underrepresented professionals have code-switched at some time or another to assimilate to a systematically white work environment. I still remember a previous manager's request that I stop wearing hoop earrings larger than the size of a quarter because clients might not perceive me as an industry leader. It was evident that she viewed hoop earrings as a "ghetto" style worn only by underqualified or unintelligent people. I wish I'd had the confidence to question her further on her request—but instead, I pretended I wasn't offended so she wouldn't feel uncomfortable.

If you do not feel like you can be entirely yourself in the workplace, you're not alone. However, good self-advocacy requires us to take proactive steps toward operating as the complete, authentic versions of ourselves at work.

Anxiety Around Image

Another contributor to the self-advocacy challenge for minorities includes anxiety around image.

Instead of making a strong case for your needs, our primary

thoughts may be, How will I be perceived by asking for this? Will they think I'm selfish? Do they value me enough to give me what I want? Suddenly, these thoughts begin to overtake the goal at hand, often discouraging us from making our request or sharing substantive and appropriate feedback.

Making Assumptions

Most professionals of color, particularly women, assume that they already know the answer to whatever they are addressing—and that answer isn't aligned with what they're advocating for. Often, this is because they have attempted to make a similar ask previously and were denied (in their current workplace or another), or the behavior and patterns of their leadership teams have demonstrated a closed approach to requests.

Alternatively, many of us can be "in our own heads" while playing out potential scenarios, assuming the worst and expecting that we will not receive what we desire.

Whatever the cause, assuming that the answer will be negative negates any chance that a breakthrough could be made.

Inability to Identify the Problem

Lastly, it can sometimes be challenging for underrepresented professionals to identify the problem at hand or the solution to whatever it is they are advocating for. This is a common challenge for most professionals I have engaged with.

Perhaps you aren't performing well at work and need to advocate for the resources to help you do your job more effectively, but you're unclear on what those resources could be. Perhaps you know you're ready for advancement and additional rewards for stellar performance or longevity at your company, but you don't know what your options are. Before you resign yourself to disappointment, take the time to research your options and know what's actually on the table.

OVERCOMING WORKPLACE TRAUMA

Taking action to advocate for yourself and build a strong personal brand requires commitment and bravery.

It's easy to say, "It should have been me." It's harder to say, "It will be me."

This switch in perspective is particularly hard for marginalized groups because it involves a degree of confrontation and vulnerability, as well as dealing with the numerous obstacles we explored above head-on.

As underrepresented professionals, we have a warranted degree of anxiety around image, visibility, and difficult conversations. As one famous study by Linda Babcock and her team at Carnegie Mellon University discovered, white men tended to liken self-advocacy at work to "playing a ball game," while other groups (in this particular study, a generalized group of women) equated it to "getting a root canal."*

While women have many reasons for avoiding conflict and self-advocacy regardless of race, for underrepresented professionals, the pain and resistance to self-advocacy and building a personal brand often comes from a very specific place: workplace trauma.

---

* *H Riley Bowles, L Babcock, L Lai. "Social incentives for gender differences in the propensity to initiate negotiations: Sometimes it does hurt to ask." Organizational Behavior and Human Decision Processes, Volume 103, Issue 1, May 2007, 84-103.*

Workplace trauma can include (but is not limited to) discrimination, racism, microaggressions, sexism, layoffs and terminations from previous roles, being passed up for opportunities, unfair treatment from leaders and peers, uncalled-for disciplinary action like performance improvement plans, and the inability to present your authentic self.

When we experience these circumstances at work, it impacts us emotionally in the moment—but what we may not realize is that it also creates a mental and emotional blueprint that can, if not addressed, follow us into every work environment thereafter. Remember how Andre struggled with putting himself forward after being belittled by his former manager? This sort of thing happens all the time.

If, in a previous role, you were placed on a performance improvement plan that you felt was unfair or unwarranted, you may experience feelings of fear or defensiveness in your current role when your manager gives you constructive criticism or cites areas of improvement. Instead of looking at these areas as an opportunity for growth, you may instead fear what's to come, and hesitate to speak out to gain more clarity or ask for support. Suddenly, instead of showing your leaders that you are capable, committed, and growth-minded, you feel like you're fighting for your job and livelihood—and all of your future conversations and decisions will be impacted by that fear.

Unfortunately, most workplaces do not have resources or support systems for transforming our inner landscapes to overwrite these old (or current) experiences. Therefore, the responsibility for transforming our responses, actions, and outcomes falls to us. Simply recognizing that you may be struggling with self-advocacy is the first step to creating major change in your career.

This book will give you the foundation for your next action steps—starting with key mindset shifts. However, you may also benefit from therapy, meditation, group work, or other well-studied modalities. Asking for help privately and finding people and groups who can support you unconditionally outside of work is a vital and necessary first step for many of us. If you aren't sure where to start, a quick Google search for culturally aware and trauma-informed therapists in your area is a great place to start.

Chapter Four

OWN YOUR NARRATIVE

WHILE I WAS WORKING for a top-ten Fortune 500 tech company, I transferred from the Silicon Valley office to the Toronto location to support the sales team as a project manager. My strong reputation and personal brand prompted my managers to write strong recommendations and position me as a perfect fit for this role. They also knew I had a strong desire to go back to my hometown, Toronto, to be closer to my aging grandmother, so this was a perfect fit.

I hit the ground running when I transferred and did everything I could to make life easier for the nearly forty sales reps and leaders on my new team. I was quickly acknowledged for going out of my way to make sure the sales teams and our clients were thriving. However, about three months after my move, a wave of depression and regret hit me. I was missing the Bay Area, specifically my mom, and felt I had made a hasty decision in moving. My mom had been a single parent all my life, and I felt like I abandoned her in a time where I could have invested back into her.

Of course, these heavy emotions affected how I showed up at work. I was still doing a great job, but for a few weeks, I retracted a bit. I wasn't as smiley as usual and kept my head down versus socializing as I typically would.

One of the leaders who reported to my manager took notice. One morning, he pulled me into a conference room. "Devika, I noticed you've been different lately."

For a split second, I thought Tom was concerned about me. I felt a rush of gratitude that I worked at a company where colleagues were invested in each other in a positive way. But his words hit me like a gut punch.

"You're not engaging with the team as much. You used to be so joyful, and the team took notice of the positivity you bring. But lately, you're not the same. I don't know what's going on, but many people would do *anything* to work here. You should be grateful to be here. If I can offer you any advice, it would be to change your attitude."

I was floored—and without knowing why, I was embarrassed. Sure, I wasn't as jovial as normal, but I wasn't walking around miserable or making the environment awkward, and I was still performing my duties well. However, my temporarily toned-down personality didn't appease Tom. I was beyond irritated that he felt privileged enough to comment on my energy, and was acting like it was my job to make the workplace more pleasant for him!

In addition to bringing this up to me—which was bad enough, since Tom and I didn't have a relationship where he should have felt comfortable approaching me in that manner—he went to my direct manager with this feedback. I know this because, later that same day, my manager passively mentioned the conversation.

Again, I was taken aback. How did I go from being recognized as a valued member of the team to "ungrateful" in just a few weeks? This experience only added to the regret I felt about moving. In my previous office, I told myself, this wouldn't have happened.

So, I did what most people would have done: I launched into "fake it 'til you make it" mode. I was still sad and regretful outside of work, but when I got to the office I slapped on a big smile and acted like the most happy, grateful person on the team.

Looking back at it, I realize this pressure to act happy through a challenging time was incredibly unhealthy. I wonder now whether Tom would have had more confidence in me if I'd had longer than just three months to show I was a strong performer and joyful contributor to the team. I simply hadn't had the time to build up a track record, gain a reputation, and own my narrative as a strong performer. Therefore, a change in how I showed up at work for a very short period of time negatively (and unfairly) impacted the way I was perceived in the long term.

There will be seasons of your career when you are struggling, barely meeting expectations of the role you're in. You may be fatigued and lacking motivation. You may be going through something in your personal life that is impacting the way you show up at work, consciously or subconsciously. This is a part of life for all professionals, in all industries—but for underrepresented professionals who already feel pressured to work twice as hard as their peers to keep their jobs and be rewarded, these completely normal seasons of challenge can feel like a huge failure. In fact, you'll be surprised how many people will take a short season of you not operating at your best and create a narrative that diminishes or overrides the excellent work you have done up until that point. People who are slow to acknowledge you as a top performer are very quick to throw negative feedback around when your performance falls even a tiny bit below expectations.

Since the experience I shared above, I've learned that time spent on a team or in a role doesn't necessarily preclude this kind of unfair behavior. You could be a rock star for years at a time, and your leaders could still flip the script and question your "fit" in the company if your performance slips even a little during a challenging season. If you're lucky enough to have a compassionate leader you can turn to and work with, that person can be a powerful ally in preserving the perception and acknowledgment of your contributions, but that isn't the reality for many underrepresented professionals. I made the mistake of employing the "fake it 'til you make it" strategy, and it was definitely harmful to both my mental health and my comfort level in the workplace in the long term. It's harder to bounce back when you have to hide what you're going through for weeks or months at a time.

The real solution is to stop letting other people control the narrative about who you are and what you bring to the table. I call this "owning your narrative."

Allowing others, especially those in decision-making or influential positions, to control or influence how others perceive you can be detrimental in two ways. The first is, of course, that seasons of low or challenging performance can be blown up to override your past successes. The second is the exact opposite.

When your leader is trying to elevate you, they are often doing so in a way that is not fully congruent with your personal goals and trajectory. For example, when I worked for a well-known professional networking platform, I was in a sales role. My manager at that time was highly supportive and wanted to ensure I excelled at the company, which I deeply appreciated. She constantly elevated my work and brand by sharing feedback with other leaders about how great I was with clients and how I consistently met and exceeded my quotas. That's glowing feedback, right? As a sales professional, you want to be known for those kinds of strengths. However, I didn't want to remain in this department. In fact, I was actively pursuing a more senior sales role in a different part of the company and needed to be known for strengths that would make me a no-brainer candidate.

In a weekly one-to-one meeting with my manager, I addressed the gap in the narrative that was being communicated about me. I said, "Thank you so much for all you do to advocate for me. I see through your actions that you want me to succeed here. But, as you know, I'd like to move into that Senior Sales role we've been discussing, and I need to be known not only for exceeding quotas but also for strategic execution and building relationships with C-Level executives. Do you agree that I have these strengths—and, if so, could you help me reinforce this narrative with decision-makers?"

My manager was more than happy to support me. In fact, she told me that the direction I gave her made her job much easier in elevating me. A few months later, when the position opened up, I ended up getting the role.

As an underrepresented professional, a narrative that is not created by you can be inhibiting. Even in the most positive situations, owning your narrative matters more than you might assume.

HOW ARE YOU KNOWN?

How do you want people to perceive your strengths and values in the workplace?

No, I'm not talking about how others want to perceive you, or even how they currently perceive you. I'm talking about how *you* want them to perceive you.

Yes, owning that narrative is possible. And it begins with understanding, defining, creating, and scaling your professional brand.

I've mentioned the term "professional brand" already in this book. So, let's really explore what that means, and how it can serve you.

You have probably heard the term "professional brand" quite often. A professional brand is an asset that can be cultivated by anyone, at any level of responsibility, in any organization.

At its heart, a professional brand is a reputation and set of values that both precede and follow you wherever you go. It will speak for you when you're not present to speak for yourself. It will shape the conversations you have before you even enter the room. And, when it's built with care and deliberation, it will make every step across that personal bridge easier, because it will inform others of how they can support you. In short, it allows you to own your narrative.

Over the course of my corporate career, I learned several approaches to creating a professional brand. Truthfully, none of them ever stuck. Most felt generic and inauthentic—like they were prepping me to say all the "right" things without really saying anything about who I was or what I wanted. They weren't customized or specific to me. As an underrepresented and historically marginalized professional, it's important to consider how your life experiences, values, and culture enhance and inform your contribution to the workplace. These factors are over and above the universal elements of personal branding and need to be considered as we shape our personal narratives. When we learn to see these factors as assets, it helps us to combat code-switching and other common challenges.

For these reasons and others, I eventually stopped searching for a perfect branding system and decided to build my own—a method I call the CISS Framework™.

CREATE YOUR AUTHENTIC PROFESSIONAL BRAND

The CISS Framework supports underrepresented professionals to develop a brand and narrative that aligns with where they've been and how it impacts them today.

CISS stands for:

- Culture contributors
- Interests
- Strengths
- Skills

Most people attempt to create their brands based on strengths and skills, but culture contributors and interests are what makes your professional brand unique. While many people might have similar strengths, educational backgrounds, and experiences to you, no one has lived your life. Your lived experiences and the things you love and value are the "something special" you bring to your company, industry, teams, and clients that can only be offered by you. They're where the magic lies, because they inform and influence your strengths and skills at every step of the way.

While the remainder of this book will be dedicated to the various aspects of building, refining, and sharing your professional brand, it all starts with your CISS Framework. Remember, you cannot expect others to meet your professional needs if you cannot communicate your own value. This framework is a great place to start exploring that.

Now, for a quick bit of advice.

Another key aspect of creating your professional brand is how you communicate your accomplishments and values using data. Most professionals talk about their successes and how they are driving value for their companies through a list of tasks or responsibilities they are actively working on or completed. This is especially true when completing self-assessments during performance evaluation cycles. Somehow, we think that a lengthy list of tasks proves how valuable we are; however, I'm here to tell you that this approach does not work. Instead, I want you to begin communicating your accomplishments and values in a themed manner, and align how what you are working on is moving the needle toward quarterly or annual team and business objectives. No matter what role you're currently in, communicating the three areas that matter the most to your leaders, and which highlight your skills and strengths, is what will help you stand out consistently. These three areas are: leadership skills, scaling solutions to business challenges, and results. I called this the LSR Method.

We'll dive further into LSR and how to communicate with leadership, scaling solutions, and results focus areas when we discuss your executive summary in Chapter Seven, but I wanted to introduce the concept now so you can add it to your thought process around your professional brand.

Identifying Your CISS

In this section, we'll look at each area of the CISS Framework and begin your process of identifying your culture contributors, interests, strengths, and skills. You can download a Google Docs worksheet for this exercise at www.devikabrij.com/thriveincolor.

Your Culture Contributors

The first part in establishing your CISS is to identify your culture contributors. Culture contributors are the factors or environments that have formed your identity and your value system. It's where you come from, and how those origins have shaped you as a person and as a professional. Culture contributors can include beliefs and faith practices, your upbringing, family expectations, and the specific culture associated with your ethnicity. More, each culture contributor can and should include a positive learning benefit or skill set associated with it.

Some examples of this could look like:

- Growing up in a single-parent household and having to learn responsibility at a very young age.
- Immigrating from your home country to your current country and developing the ability to adapt to changing environments, languages, and cultures.
- Being a caretaker or financial provider for a family member, which has enhanced your leadership style.
- Being committed to your faith practice, which has influenced how you engage with your colleagues and those in more senior positions.

- Playing competitive sports growing up, which imparted discipline and shaped your ability to be a team player.

The goal here is to understand how your culture contributors influence the way you show up as a professional in the workplace.

You may be asking, why does this matter? To answer that question, I'll share a personal example with you.

I am the youngest daughter of a single mother who raised my sisters and I in Silicon Valley, one of the most expensive areas in the world. My mom was very intentional about stretching every dollar to provide for three growing girls on one income. Growing up, I watched her use Excel spreadsheets to budget effectively and account for every penny.

When I became a manager and received my quarterly budget for my team, I integrated the same budget planning methods I saw growing up to ensure my team got the most possible value from our team budget. This wasn't something I chose to do intentionally; rather, it was organic based on the way I learned how to manage money by observing my mother. My leaders took notice of how mindful I was with company money. It became a joke and expectation that "Devika will be the last to submit her budget." It was true. While other managers were more fluid with how they decided to spend team funds, I chose to be extra strategic. Though they poked fun at me, they identified me as a person of high integrity whom they could trust with company resources.

So, this seemingly unrelated aspect of my upbringing played a major role in how I showed up as a leader in the workplace. More, it elevated my brand and influenced how people saw me—someone who was intentional and could be trusted with company resources.

Your personal experiences and background contribute to how you show up in the workplace whether you realize it or not. Taking the time to understand your personal culture contributors—and, specifically, how those factors drive a positive outcome for your team and company—is an empowering action because it helps you identify the complete picture of your professional worth and mitigates imposter syndrome. Moreover, it creates an authentic narrative, created by you, that others can celebrate and share.

So, I invite you to take a moment to pause, download the CISS Worksheet at www.devikabrij.com/thriveincolor (or pull out your paper journal), and write down three to five of your culture contributors. As you think about your accomplishments and the values you contribute to your team, company, clients, and stakeholders, I want you to anchor into the "why" behind the awesome professional you are.

Your Interests

The second part of your CISS is your interests. These are the things that make you feel energetic, motivated, and fulfilled both at work and outside of work.

It's important for you to be aware of your interests, and for your leaders and teams to know about them as well. This will help you to create space to integrate them into your work life and also set an expectation that you will prioritize these areas outside of work.

Here's a short list of possible interests to spark your thought process:

- Travel
- Mentoring others

- Spending time with loved ones
- Volunteering
- Being involved in your place of worship
- Public speaking (both in person and virtual)
- Playing a sport
- Podcasting
- Writing (journaling, articles, or books)
- Planning social events
- Creating online content

When your leaders and team know your interests, a number of things will change. First, you seem more human, and they will learn new ways of relating to you. Second, they won't be taken by surprise when you integrate these pieces of yourself into the workplace. Third, your interests can help you create opportunities. For example, as someone who often volunteers outside of work, you could share why contributing to the company's vision for diversity and inclusion by leading an employee resource group is something you are passionate about and want to create space for. If there are company initiatives that align with your areas of interest, sharing your interests with leaders ahead of time can help you get selected for those opportunities and keep your work feeling fun and stimulating.

Finally, communicating your interests sets an expectation and precedent that these things will be integrated into your work life, which supports setting boundaries. This is especially important for underrepresented individuals, particularly women, who often fear the perception of not being committed enough to their work responsibilities. A personal interest of mine is attending a mid-week gathering at my church to engage in community and deepen my relationship with my faith. I made it a point to let my manager and teams know that if there was a team dinner, event, or work travel on a Wednesday evening, it was likely that I would not be present. Setting expectations and boundaries with my team and leaders from the beginning saved me a lot of frustration and anxiety.

What are your interests both within and outside of work? Take a moment to jot these down, even if you can't yet see how they relate to your work life.

Strengths and Skills

Now, I want you to identify your strengths and skills—by which I mean the areas of personality and action in which you are known to excel.

I define strengths as inherent or natural qualities—personal attributes that contribute to your ability to operate effectively. For example, you might have strengths in leadership, problem-solving, communication, or strategic thinking. On the other hand, skills are learned abilities that individuals acquire over time through training, education, and experience.

Here are just a few examples of strengths and skills:

- Strategy
- Effective communication
- Leading with empathy
- Effectively presenting solutions to drive business forward
- Excellent customer service or management skills
- Optimizing inefficient processes

- Organization
- Developing processes and systems
- Fostering a collaborative and trusting work environment
- Working effectively under pressure
- Technical skills
- Data analysis

Depending on your role, the above examples may or may not resonate with you, but I hope they get your wheels turning.

For this exercise, I want you to think of the strengths and skills that are relevant to your job—and, specifically, the skills you are measured on in performance evaluations and job interviews. Moreover, I want you to think about the skills and strengths that bring you energy, because if you are associated with certain skills and strengths by your leadership team, you are likely to get pulled into work that leverages those skills. If you do not enjoy those types of work, you are bound to feel depleted, frustrated, and resentful toward your job and leaders. Just because you are good at something doesn't mean you love it! For example, I am a great event planner at small to medium scales, but I absolutely loathe the process. Because I knew my strengths and skills and was clear on what I did and did not want to do, I ended up leaving a job where I was constantly asked to plan events despite the fact that it was not a core expectation of my role when I was hired.

Now, list your strengths and skills to complete your CISS. As you identify your strengths and skills, ensure that at least half of them bring you energy, passion, and joy.

PUTTING YOUR CISS TO WORK

As you complete your CISS, please take your time and be intentional instead of rushing through. We'll be using this data for the frameworks you will create in the upcoming chapters, including creating your elevator pitch, communicating with leadership, scaling solutions, and results foci.

To recap, identifying your CISS enables you to:

- Know your professional brand.
- Understand how your specific and unique characteristics make you valuable as a professional.
- Inspire leaders, peers, mentors, and sponsors to advocate for you.
- Establish your narrative on your own terms
- Understand what you value in life, including your negotiables and non-negotiables.

You bring something unique to your company, team, and role, and it's your responsibility to demonstrate that authentically. Never assume that your leaders and peers see your complete, authentic value for themselves. You need to show them and remind them consistently. This is part of coming to the table as an empowered professional.

After you have established your CISS, consider sharing it with your managers, mentors, and sponsors. No, you don't need to bust out your notebook and show them what you've written under each category, but providing visibility around what you've identified will inform others about how they can best support you. So, in your next one-to-one with your manager, mentor, or sponsor, mention that you've been reading this book and are taking steps to be more intentional about your career. Share with them what you learned through the CISS reflection and what it has shown you about your brand within the team and company.

Below is a script to help you position this effectively:

"Hi, [insert manager's name],

As you may know, I've been thinking about my career and how I'd like to approach my professional development. I'm currently reading a book about the importance of creating a professional brand. The author introduced the concept of identifying how our life experiences, interests, strengths, and skills impact how we approach our work.

I'd like to share the experiences, interests, strengths, and skills I identified with you so we can collaborate on opportunities and projects that would be a great fit for me. Are you open to hearing what I identified through this helpful exercise? I'd appreciate your feedback on how we can keep these areas in mind as we think about my development here at [insert company name]."

Thank you,
[Your signoff]

You may be thinking, "Devika, why would my manager care?" Trust me, they will. By proactively leading this discussion, you are taking the guesswork out of how they can support your developmental needs. You aren't asking for anything that requires heavy lifting from your manager (like a raise or promotion); you're simply giving them data on how to best support you in a way that is rooted in your proactive thinking. By taking this initiative, you're making the task of management easier on your leader while showing them that you are invested in your own growth. That speaks volumes.

As you grow in your career and acquire different experiences, your CISS will change. I suggest updating your CISS twice a year. The great thing is, this framework will always be a relevant way to understand the core of your professional brand as you develop and grow. Each time you update, approach the process thoughtfully, and share your results with your leadership.

Chapter Five

MINDSET MATTERS

FOR MOST OF my life, I genuinely believed I was stupid.

Throughout my school years and several years into my career, I operated as if this was true. As a young child, I was called stupid in arguments with young family members, and my child's mind could not separate the insult from my reality. This belief was strengthened when adults I trusted compared me unfavorably to other children.

I clearly remember my father taking me to a friend's house. This girl was incredibly good at math, while I did better in English and history. While she and I played, my father and hers would give us impromptu math quizzes. Even if I knew the answer, my friend was faster. I could see how impressed my father was with my friend—and even though he didn't say anything to me explicitly, I knew he was disappointed in my performance.

I did well in school and was accepted to AP (advanced placement) classes in high school, but I never achieved higher than a 3.8

GPA. I got into my first-choice university, but not into most others I applied to. Even though, from the outside, it appeared I was doing quite well, I felt like I was constantly underachieving.

"Good," in my world, wasn't good *enough.*

When I was hired by influential companies like Google and LinkedIn, I never felt smart enough to be there. I was terrified to speak up in meetings with my peers and clients because I truly believed everyone would laugh at my ideas. My heart would race if someone asked me for my opinion in front of my team. It was like being with my math-whiz friend all over again. I internalized every piece of negative feedback, and brushed aside sincere compliments, thinking, "They're just trying to make me feel like I belong here even though they know I don't."

Your mindset is like a massive tree growing through the center of your life. Its roots are often in childhood, but its branches touch everything in your world. Whatever foundational beliefs, expectations, and worldviews were planted as seeds by your upbringing and experiences are now impacting your life. If you keep watering that tree, it will keep bearing fruit—even if that fruit is poisoning you.

WHAT IS "MINDSET," ANYWAY?

What you believe about yourself ultimately impacts your success or failure. Only you can determine what you believe—and therefore, what your "mindset" is.

Of course, it would be easy to think the most positive thoughts and expect the best outcomes if we never had to face the disappointment, fear, rejection, and doubt triggered by situations outside of our control. But, since expecting a smooth ride all the time is unrealistic, we can develop coping mechanisms and personal practices that protect our mindset from outside influences and keep our thoughts centered on what *we* decide is important.

When I started to pay attention to how my own mindset was affecting my experience at work, I got curious. I couldn't be the only person struggling with self-doubt and thoughts of being unqualified! I began to study the influential leaders around me and how they operated to create their own versions of success. I noticed that many of them, regardless of age, faith, race, or life experience, called out something specific when asked about their path to success.

That specific thing was "manifestation."

Now, if you're anything like I was, the word "manifestation" makes you cringe. If you're a realist and highly analytical, the thought of "creating" reality based on your thoughts probably seems unreasonable, even insane. However, when I replaced the word "manifestation" with the word "faith," it all made sense to me.

Even as a realist, I've always had a personal relationship with God, and believe that God hears the prayers of my heart. I have a track record of getting my needs met, even when things seem impossible. Sure, the timing sometimes hasn't been what I expected, and sometimes my needs were met in a totally different way than I'd imagined, but my prayers have always been answered.

Now, to the important part: I know now that my prayers were answered because I *believed* they would be answered. I believed in the outcome despite my lack of power, poor choices, and unfair circumstances. That level of belief was, and is, faith.

The Bible describes faith as "being sure of what we hope for, and certain of what we do not see." (Hebrews 11)

If that doesn't resonate, you can replace "faith" with "trust" or "knowing." When we operate from this place of innate trust and knowing, we create opportunities for ourselves to receive a different outcome.

Your mindset, in essence, is composed of the things you believe, trust, and have faith in. When you "know" something is true, you will operate in every aspect of your life *as though that thing is true.* The people in my world who *believe* and *know* God will carry them through everything often experience synchronicities and even miracles that no one, including them, can explain. The people who *believe* and *know* that they will get a promotion get the promotion, even against incredible odds. The people who *believe* and *know* that they will become leaders eventually become leaders.

And the people who believe they are stupid, unworthy, or underprepared, like I used to? They end up making decisions, responding to opportunities, and conducting conversations *as if those things were true.*

In order to change my mindset and release its stranglehold on my personal and professional life, I needed to adopt, rehearse, and implement a new, more positive mindset. I needed to decide on a new set of expectations for myself that felt more aligned with where I wanted to be in my career. Then, I needed to flex my faith muscles, use my imagination, and operate *as if this new set of beliefs were true* until I started seeing evidence that they were, in fact, true.

There's actually a lot of research behind this approach. Thoughts, like other habits, create well-worn neural pathways in the brain. When situations trigger our insecurities or fears, our thoughts gravitate toward the most common pathways—those we've worn over time through repetitive thoughts. Me repeating to myself, "I'm so stupid!" created a default neural pathway to which

I returned over and over again, even when there was no real "evidence" that the thought was true.

I started deliberately working on my mindset a few years into my career. I felt like I was making progress. I learned to stop the spiral into self-recrimination when I was offered constructive criticism. I hadn't completely mastered my insecurities (I still haven't, to be honest), but I was making good progress.

Then, in 2012, I was offered a job at the Silicon Valley headquarters of one of the world's largest tech companies. At that point, most of my roles had been in the entertainment space, so I had minimal experience in tech, but I was beyond excited to be there. I'd been hired as a project manager to create and build a system for tracking expired work visas and ensure that all employees working in the United States were compliant with immigration law. This project would be scaled across every office in the country. Thankfully, I'd learned this exact process in my former company, and was able to easily create and replicate a functional system. In doing so, I saved the company millions of dollars in fees and legal expenses.

For the first time in my life, I was confident that I had the expertise and know-how to be exactly where I was. When the company decided to expand its Toronto office, I took the opportunity to return to the city of my birth and work alongside a highly influential female executive whom I respected and admired. My role was to be this leader's right hand and manage several initiatives to help her, her teams, their clients, and the greater sales organization scale success and become Canada's leading advertising brand. I couldn't have been happier.

I soon discovered, however, that this new role was too vague and had minimal parameters around expectations. I knew I was expected to be flexible and nimble to meet the various demands of the team, but many of the major initiatives did not fit my experience and expertise—such as planning high-visibility, industry-wide events with thousands of attendees, or building a website for newly hired sales executives to streamline their onboarding. These responsibilities felt crippling because of their importance and visibility; I knew that, even if I tried my hardest and worked myself to the brink of exhaustion, there was no way I could succeed. No amount of research could make me an instant expert in the various fields I was supposed to oversee.

The pressure was enormous. And, though I did my best (and then some), I just couldn't cut it. Nor did I feel comfortable with my new manager, especially once I sensed her disappointment. Immediately, my old thoughts kicked in: "See, Devika? You don't belong here."

A year into the role, I decided to move to a new company and position.

I can see now that the expectations for this role were not realistic. We needed three highly capable people to execute the tasks that had been delegated to me alone. But at the time, I couldn't see and accept that no one, no matter how qualified, could have succeeded in my position.

In my next role, my insecurities came back around to bite me. I'd been in my position for about a year when my peers began nudging me to apply for a role that would soon become vacant.

"You think I'm ready for *that*?" I asked. "I just got here! I'm still learning a new industry!"

But my colleagues were confident, and I realized that all of my doubt and hesitation was coming from inside myself, not from those around me. My experience in my previous role had brought it all up again, but ultimately, it was my own lack of confidence as much as the role itself that had undermined my success.

So, I decided that I would approach this interview as though I already had the job. I would have faith that, if I really was the best person for the role, I would get the job.

I interviewed for the role a few weeks later. And I got it.

Soon after, I came across an episode of Oprah's *Super Soul Sunday* where she spoke about how manifestation—aka, belief—created her success, impact, and influence. "The way you think creates reality for yourself," she stated while sharing about the abuse she endured as a child. She took the necessary steps to change her thoughts in pursuit of her professional dreams. She knew that it was what she believed, not what others thought, that would ultimately determine her success or failure.

That's when it all clicked for me. My fears of being perceived as stupid were the biggest obstacle inhibiting me from reaching my potential. More, my beliefs—and the actions I took because I believed them—were inhibiting *other people* from seeing my potential. How could I expect others to believe in me when I didn't even believe in myself?

At that moment, I realized that the seeds of doubt, insecurity, and comparison planted in my childhood had become a giant sequoia tree in my life. If I wanted a different experience, I needed to stop watering the meritless narrative I had created for myself, and turn my attention elsewhere. It was time for me to adopt the truth of who I was: a smart, capable, and worthy woman who had inherited the strength of generations of ancestors from multiple nationalities, races, and experiences. I knew that, if I could believe this about myself, I would be unstoppable.

I started putting in the work to recreate my thoughts toward myself. At first, I had no evidence that my new beliefs were true;

that was where my faith came in. I needed to believe in something I couldn't yet see so I could usher in that new way of being.

When the seeds of this new truth began to take root within me, everything changed. I no longer accepted the unacceptable. I advocated for myself and my aspirations. I owned up to my shortcomings without the burden of shame. I stopped overachieving to try to prove I wasn't stupid.

You can do the same. Right now. Today.

BELIEVE BIGGER

"My manager should know the great work I do. My performance speaks for itself. If I keep going like this, I'll definitely get the promotion I asked for."

Jaden, who would eventually become my client, was confident that his commitment and quality of work were self-evident. This confidence was rooted in his Nigerian upbringing and culture, which told him to be grateful for any opportunity that came his way, stay humble (because so many people like him would give *anything* to be in his position), work extra hard (because leadership was bound to notice), and stay the course through any adversity.

However, as we've learned, this approach rarely works as planned for underrepresented professionals.

Jaden worked at a globally recognized finance company for over two years before he realized that he had outgrown his role. He was no longer feeling challenged, and because he hadn't negotiated his salary when he accepted the role, he was also underpaid. Getting *any* opportunity in a company as recognized as this one had been his main objective when he accepted the position; in his mind, just having this company on his resume would open multiple doors for him throughout his career.

"Just stick with it," his parents assured him. "If you work twice as hard as everyone else, you'll eventually get to where you want to be." But working twice as hard as his peers for less money than they were commanding no longer felt like the right approach, and Jaden was getting frustrated.

As we learned in Chapter One, the well-meaning beliefs we inherit from our parents and cultures can hinder us in our professional environments. All aspects of our identities as underrepresented professionals—including our cultures, faith backgrounds, and ethnic ideologies, as well as our unique personal and professional experiences—shape how we show up in our careers. But many of those inherited beliefs and patterns were shaped by parents, grandparents, and ancestors who had a very different experience of both work and life than we do.

As a person of color, you have probably had toxic words spoken to—or over—you countless times. Some of them, you may have unknowingly adopted as truth. All of your experiences of unfair treatment and rejection in the workplace have reinforced those beliefs and fractured your identity. While there's nothing we can do to change the past, or how other people choose to receive us, I'm asking you to believe bigger about our future—and that starts with your mindset.

Until you get your mind right, you will keep watering the same old tree. More, you will hold yourself back from opportunities that you deserve and are worthy of, all because of how you see yourself.

PRAISE DOES NOT EQUAL PROMOTION

Too many people like Jaden—top performers who work twice as hard as their white counterparts—don't receive the recognition and compensation they deserve. And unless they adopt the mindset of self-belief that allows them to actually advocate for their advancement, they probably never will.

Jaden was constantly praised by his team—but praise without promotion is meaningless in the long run. He wanted more, and when he didn't receive it, his positive view of the company he'd been so excited to join started to shift. He knew where he wanted to be in his career, but the right doors simply weren't opening.

Ultimately, he decided to leave the company, but the cycle of overwork and under-promotion followed him to every position he took. Soon, he came to *expect* that he'd get shot down when he asked for a promotion. He was in the "Gap"—the vague place of transition between his comfort zone and the "something greater" he felt called to in his career.

It was at that point that he and I started working together.

The Gap is a common place where people slip into the 3D Cycle I shared in Chapter One. It's also a place where the truth of our mindset reveals itself. The discontentment, defeat, and doubt of the 3D Cycle are produced not just by our circumstances at work but by *how we have been conditioned to think about and relate to those circumstances.*

The great Civil Rights-era activist Rosa Parks once said, "I have learned over the years that, when one's mind is made up, this diminishes fear." While I'm sure this mindset was amazingly motivating for her, I'm also sure that there must have been times when she didn't feel that way—when she felt defeated by the sheer scale of the fight. I've found that the same is true for me, and for most of the Black, Indigenous, and other people of color I've worked with over the years. The challenges we experience in our workplaces, especially those influenced by inherent bias, discrimination, and racism, cause mental calluses that, slowly and over time, inhibit us from seeing ourselves as prepared and worthy to receive what we're working toward. These beliefs and attitudes, perhaps more than anything we actually do (or don't do) at work, make it harder to reach our potential.

No matter how challenging it is, we *must* find a way to create the inner certainty that Ms. Parks spoke of—and keep coming back to it, over and over, even when we are in the Gap.

In other words, we need to *believe*. We need to have *faith*. And we need to proceed as if we deserve and will ultimately receive what we desire.

Don't worry, I'm not about to launch into a fluffy "thoughts are things" diatribe or start lecturing you about how you need to keep your vibration high in order to create the life and career you desire. I find that approach unhelpful at best, and abusive at worst. However, we cannot progress into the prescriptive strategies and advancement tools in this book without doing the work to reset our belief patterns.

Mastering your mind is mission-critical to attaining your career goals over time. Without the skills to redirect your thoughts toward problem-solving, leverage your failures as learning experiences, and retain your self-confidence in the face of opposition, you will almost certainly end up battling 3D feelings. However, when you understand how to make your mind work for you at work, you will be able to leverage the tools in this book to get that promotion, make more money, communicate effectively with leadership, move into more senior roles, and create the career path you truly desire and deserve.

Are you ready to get your mind right?

FOUR STEPS TO TRANSFORMING YOUR MINDSET

Mastering your mind is as intimidating as it can be motivating. It may feel, sometimes, as if your thoughts and feelings are beyond your ability to control. However, I can promise you that taking these simple, intentional, evidence-based steps with consistency will change your mindset—and, by extension, your life.

You can apply these steps in any challenging circumstance that causes you to slip into unhealthy thought patterns.

Step 1: Reflect on What Was Said

The first step in getting your mind right is reflecting on the negative words that have been inflicted on you (intentionally or unintentionally) through the disappointments, doubts, rejection, and fears of others. These words have (consciously or unconsciously) fractured how you see yourself and your ability to create the personal and professional life you desire.

Grab a journal and write whatever comes to mind about any negative or inhibiting experiences that you are carrying from your past. What words were said to you that fractured the way you see your intelligence, self-worth, confidence, or expectations for yourself? Be specific and detailed.

For example, perhaps you heard some (or many) of the following:

- "You're so stupid."
- "Be grateful for what you have, and don't ask for more."
- "You'll never get that job."
- "You'll never earn that much money."
- "You're asking too much."
- "You don't belong here."
- "You're not ready."
- "You're not a good fit."
- "You'll never make it."
- "That isn't for people like us."

Step 2: Reflect on What Happened

List out all of the experiences that have negatively impacted your career, inhibited your confidence, or stopped you from pursuing what you desire. For example:

- "I was fired for 'poor performance.'"
- "I didn't get the job because I was 'asking for too much.'"
- "I worked long hours trying to prove myself, and never spent time with my family. Then, my parent died, and I never got to say goodbye. I feel so guilty that I've stopped pursuing my dreams."
- "I was blindsided by a horrible performance review."

- "I was paid 30 percent less than my white colleague for the same job."
- "I was called defensive and angry for asking questions and expressing feedback."
- "I was told to eliminate my accent if I wanted to be successful."
- "I was repeatedly told 'no' when asking for a promotion or salary increase."
- "I disappointed my family when I chose a career outside their expectations."
- "I stumble every time I try to stand up to those in authority."
- "My white peer who performed less well than me was promoted over me, and I gave up."
- "My family started treating me differently when I reached levels of success."

Step 3: Flip the Script

Now that you know what to look for, you can probably see how your experiences fed your mindset, and how your mindset fed your experiences. Take a moment to sit with what comes up for you around that. How does it feel to see the connection?

Now comes the critical part. Please write down the *opposites* of the negative words and experiences you identified in Steps One and Two.

For example, if you identified, "You're so stupid!" under Step 1, cross it out and write down, "I am intelligent. People desire to hear my ideas and feedback." If you identified, "I didn't get the job because I was asking for too much," write down, "I ask for what I deserve and am confident that it will be given to me."

Create positive opposite affirmations for every example in the first two steps of this exercise. Don't leave any of them out! Then, write out a clean copy of your positive statements and place it where you will see it daily—like on your nightstand, your bathroom mirror, your desk, or next to your coffee maker. Read them aloud every day.

This might feel weird at first, but this action step will challenge your brain to adopt a new, real, positive narrative about yourself. You must create awareness, become intentional, and retrain your brain before you can achieve career transformation. In essence, you are planting a new seed, watering it, and allowing it to grow. If you abandon the new seed a few days into the process, you will stunt its growth.

This process is backed by research. Dr. Jacob Towery, Adjunct Clinical Instructor in the Department of Psychiatry at Stanford University, confirms that, "The brain is neuroplastic, meaning neural networks can continue to grow, change, and reorganize throughout the lifespan. By challenging yourself with new experiences and perspectives, you can form new neural connections—or mindsets—at any point in life … The exciting news about mindsets is that they are absolutely changeable. The entire field of cognitive therapy is based on the idea that thoughts determine feelings and that you can learn powerful techniques to modify distorted thoughts and self-defeating beliefs."*

Nothing about our mindset is set in stone. No matter who said what to you, or what negative or hurtful experiences you've been

---

**Primeau, Mia. " Your powerful, changeable mindset." Stanford Report, September 15, 2021. https://news.stanford.edu/report/2021/09/15/mindsets-clearing-lens-life/*

through, I'm here to assure you that you have the power to change your internal landscape.

Shifting your mindset will not happen overnight. It will take consistency and many weeks or months of rehearsing the truth of who you are and what you deserve through positive affirmations and deliberately redirecting your mind. However, both you and I know that you—and your future—are worth the effort.

Step 4: Forgive the Ones Who Hurt You

Yes, you read that right. Your final action step is to forgive and celebrate others.

Whether the people around you intended to inflict their own insecurities, prejudices, and lack of imagination on you or not, you can choose to forgive them for their actions. I'm not asking you to forget what happened, excuse the harm that was done, or reestablish relationships that no longer serve you—only to release the anger, resentment, and frustration you're carrying, because that's affecting you, not them.

There's a common saying I've held on to throughout my life: "Harboring unforgiveness is like drinking poison and hoping the person who hurt you will die." This bit of wisdom has helped me remember that forgiveness is for my own good, which has helped me process and let go of unfair and hurtful experiences in the workplace. The people who have hurt you deeply, whether they take accountability or not, will move forward in their lives without much concern to how you've been impacted. By holding these harmful experiences close to you, the only one you're hurting is you.

Sometimes, forgiveness can happen in an instant; other times, it takes years. But the first step in forgiveness is always the choice to forgive—and that choice is yours and yours alone.

I'd like to guide you through the steps I've taken, and have helped my clients take, that has helped move the needle in forgiveness. So, grab your journal, and let's go.

- *Write down the name of the person you need to forgive.* Of course, you can include people in your personal circle, but for this exercise, I want you to focus on managers, colleagues, mentors, or anyone who has done something wrong against you. Now, write, "[Insert name here], I choose to forgive you."
- *Recall the hurt, disappointment, anger, and other emotions because of this person's words or actions.* You might be wondering, "Why would I want to bring up those feelings again?" but you owe it to yourself to be honest about how you've been impacted. Write down all the feelings that come up for you.
- *Write down the events that occurred as a result of the person's words or actions.* For example, perhaps you were wrongfully terminated and struggled to find a new job for a year, which impacted your finances and confidence. Perhaps a peer provided poor feedback to your manager during a performance review which inhibited your shot at promotion. Draw a line between the person's words or actions and the result.
- *Find gratitude for what happened.* This one always gets me side-eye, but it's important. What have you learned as a result of these events that you didn't know before? Did the hurtful situation actually end up working out for the good? For example, perhaps

after that wrongful termination pushed you out of the company you found a job at a company you're much happier with. Perhaps the missed promotion worked in your favor because the additional workload and pressure would have been problematic for your work/life balance. Perhaps you simply learned what type of peer or leader you never want to be. Identify the enlightenment, lesson, or favor that resulted from that person's wrong toward you, and write it down.

- *Step into forgiveness.* After you've acknowledged, unpacked, and practiced gratitude, you're in an effective space to let go of the person who wronged you. You don't need to have a conversation with them to tell them they are forgiven (unless you want to), or allow them back into your life if their season with you is over. This forgiveness is for you, and it will release you to move forward in power, maturity, and grace.

Step 5: Celebrate the Ones You Admire

Once you've completed the exercise in Step Four (and you may need to do it multiple times to find forgiveness for multiple people), it's time to celebrate those around you who have achieved the success you desire.

In the age of social media, insecurities are at an all-time high. If you're feeling stuck, unmotivated, or unaccomplished, seeing the Instagram-glossy success of those around you can feel like a slap in the face. This is especially true when we see those who haven't worked as hard as we have, or for as long, getting the rewards we desire for ourselves.

As an underrepresented professional, you've likely seen this more times than you can count. In fact, feeling unappreciated is a primary reason why 79 percent of employees in the United States leave their jobs. In fact, 65 percent of employees say they've received no recognition in the past twelve months!* While the data doesn't divide these statistics by race, I'd hazard a guess that those numbers are even higher for professionals of color. That said, seeing others' successes as your failures is a mindset trap. Spending your mental energy on envy and frustration may feel vindicating in the moment, but it won't help you in the long term. Instead, celebrate the people who have already attained what you want. Celebrate your friends, your colleagues, and even your bosses. Being genuinely happy for those around you will position you to attract good things, too. Your time is coming—and you are worthy of celebrating, too.

Here are some easy ways to celebrate people in your world:

- Send a handwritten congratulatory note whenever someone in your department is promoted. Express your excitement for them and share one thing you think they're doing really well.
- Coordinate a team e-card for someone who accepted a job at a different company.
- Publicly recognize the successes of your peers or team leader(s) during key meetings or on LinkedIn.

---

* *"10 Ways to Ensure All Your Employees Feel Valued and Appreciated at Work." O.C. Tanner, https://www.octanner.com/articles/10-ways-to-ensure-all-your-employees-feel-valued-and-appreciated-at-work*

Like every other step in changing your mindset, celebrating others takes practice. However, when you do it authentically, it creates space for good things to happen for you, too. Call it God, karma, or whatever you like—it works.

MOVING ON

Shifting your mindset through authentic reflection, flipping the script, forgiving those who have hurt you, and celebrating others will help you in ways you can't even imagine right now. Your mastery of your inner landscape will help you create the career and life you truly desire—and to know the difference between what is true for you and what is simply something you were told.

I'm happy to say that Jaden, after implementing the steps in this chapter, eventually found a fulfilling role at a company that valued and properly incentivized him. This work required him to challenge many of the roots of his identity—in particular, his family narrative about work and recognition—but once he did, he was able to create a strong personal brand, advocate for himself in powerful ways, and say no to what was not right for him.

You are more than your negative experiences. You are more than the seeds others planted in your mind. Make the choice now not to let your past dictate your future, and you'll position yourself to win.

Chapter Six

YOUR ELEVATOR PITCH

JOANNA WAS A FEW years into working at a well-known online food ordering company when, while visiting the company's Chicago office to meet with her team, she stepped into the kitchen to fill her water bottle. A moment later, Mike, a company executive for whom she had a lot of respect, walked in and headed for the snack wall.

"Are you a chip fan?" he asked. "Any recommendations?"

Joanna, unused to running into executives outside of formal meetings, was caught by surprise. "This office has a *lot* of snack options compared to mine, so I can see why it's a challenging choice."

"Are you visiting from another office?"

"Yes, I work remotely from San Diego. Some of my team members are in this office so I'm here to meet with them."

"I'm Mike." He offered his hand to shake. "What's your name? What do you do here?"

"I'm Joanna. I'm a Relationship Manager with the Customer Partnerships team."

"Very cool. Well, enjoy your stay!"

Joanna wasn't one to glorify executives and leaders. In fact, we often spoke about how cringy it was when people who worked at the company asked for selfies with the CEO and other executives only to post them on LinkedIn as if they were major celebrities. But for Joanna, meeting Mike was cool because she had developed respect for him over her years with the company. She had observed him from afar during company-wide meetings and appreciated his clear communication, authentic demeanor, and laid-back approach. He had a way of making everyone feel seen and heard.

Mike was someone Joanna would have loved to have as a sponsor, or at least as a mentor she could learn from. The idea wasn't far-fetched, given that Mike was a senior leader across the line of business within which she worked. He had incredible experience in growing relationships with customers, and Joanna's vision for her career trajectory mirrored his in many ways. In fact, Mike had been a remote employee for over five years during his own corporate climb. Having struggled to remain visible with leaders with barely any face time with the team, Joanna knew that well-placed support within the organization could make a world of difference.

After telling me the story of her chance encounter with Mike, Joanna shared that she was immediately disappointed in herself. "I do so much for this company's highest revenue-driving customers. I know Mike hears about that and probably doesn't realize it's me managing those relationships. Why didn't I bring that up? It could have led to a conversation where I could have fostered rapport and potentially furthered a mentoring relationship. I'm so *annoyed* with myself, Devika!"

I'll bet you've been in Joanna's situation at least once. At networking events, during interviews, or even in social settings, the conversation opener is often "What do you do?" or "Tell me about yourself." If you're anything like most people, you'll probably state your title and the organization you work for: "I'm a Marketing Manager for Coca-Cola," or, "I'm a Digital Customer Experience Director for Eddie Bauer."

Most of the time, the response will simply be, "Nice." Or maybe, "Wow, that's cool." And then, the conversation will move on. Why do you think that is?

Unless you've made it to the C-suite, where the "C" usually speaks for itself, your title is unlikely to explain the value you're driving in your day-to-day role. Since you've given no real information about your skills, your strengths, or even your role beyond the title, the only way for people to respond is "Nice." It's a bland answer for a bland statement.

Now, imagine what could be different if your answer to conversational questions conveyed the depth of your work and your pride in what you spend your days doing. Imagine the opportunities that would open up if you could be seen for your true contribution in the first few minutes of a conversation!

That's what happened to me.

I was completely bored with my role at an entertainment company when I decided to distract myself from my discouragement and frustration by attending an acquaintance's birthday party. I hardly knew anyone there, so I was doing the whole song and dance of meeting people for the first time. A woman named Lisa asked me the token question: "What do you do?"

"I work in Human Resources," I replied. "Specifically, I work within the Global Mobility team. I'm building a system to track employees who are on visas to ensure their work permits are current so the company isn't fined and their employment with us isn't jeopardized."

Lisa raised her eyebrows. "That must be a hot job right now. My roommate is looking for someone who does something similar. She works for Google."

Of course, my eyes lit up immediately. Growing up in Silicon Valley, one of the largest tech hubs in the world, a job at Google was a dream.

"Lisa, I know we just met, but ... would you mind introducing me to your roommate? I'd love to learn more about that role if she's open to it. I'm actually in the market for a new opportunity."

Lisa was happy to do so. Long story short, Lisa connected me to her roommate via email, we spoke, I went through what felt like 1,000 interviews, and I got the job. More, it ended up being one of the most fulfilling roles in my corporate career. It also pivoted me from working at a company where I was undervalued to a path in tech that brought me even bigger opportunities.

What would have happened if I had met Lisa's question with, "Oh, I work in HR"?

Whether it's creating connections with people you admire, positioning yourself to stand out in an interview process, seeking out new opportunities, or simply having productive conversations at networking events, owning and articulating your professional narrative matters.

Most of the time, opportunities come not because you're chasing them, but because you're in the right place at the right time. Being prepared and well-positioned can open doors you may not have considered. If Joanna had more clearly communicated her responsibilities and value to the team to Mike, she potentially could have accessed a follow-up conversation—especially because he was the type of person who would be willing to foster a deeper dialogue.

Situations like the ones above happen more often than you might realize. If you can't clearly articulate your value and contributions, you cannot expect others to understand and act on them.

WHAT STORY ARE YOU TELLING?

In this chapter, we'll explore one key aspect of owning your narrative: your elevator pitch. This is a key verbal component of your narrative that has all kinds of useful applications.

But first, let's define what it means to "own your narrative."

Your "narrative," in the context of your career and personal brand, is your self-created, concise, and comprehensive story that describes the overall value you drive within and outside of your role, and across your team, your direct organization, and your company as a whole. It includes your key accomplishments and the professional brand you are known for (or want to be known for).

The goal of creating your narrative is to quickly and clearly connect the dots between your day-to-day responsibilities and the business or team objectives your leaders identify over the course of every quarter and year. Your narrative will then become a tool to support you in your communication in professional environments, especially with decision-makers and with those who are auditory (versus visual) learners.

When I work with clients around owning their narratives, their first response is usually confusion. Often, they've never been asked to frame their contributions in this way. However—and this is vitally important—*a confused messenger creates a confused message.*

If you are confused or unclear about the narrative that will best represent your professional brand and your expectations for your career, you will also confuse the people who are listening to you.

In this chapter, we will take a big leap toward clear messaging through the framework of your *elevator pitch.* This framework will support you to establish your narrative and articulate it clearly, without hesitation or awkwardness, in numerous professional settings.

What Is an Elevator Pitch?

If you cannot boldly own and express your value, you cannot expect others to understand your value or advocate for you.

On the other hand, when you can succinctly convey exactly what you do, what you stand for, and the value you drive, you will gain the confidence to make requests, gain buy-in from mentors and sponsors, and position yourself for greater opportunities.

How empowered would you feel if you could clearly and confidently articulate your professional value while tying in aspects of your personal life that give a full picture of who you are? Would an exchange between you and the next person who asks, "What do you do?" feel more connected versus transactional? What would it do to alleviate your imposter syndrome? Would it open up opportunities you didn't expect?

Those are just a few reasons why you need a great elevator pitch.

I'm sure you've heard the term "elevator pitch" before, but you may not have understood what goes into it, how to create it, or when to use it. So, let's start there.

Your elevator pitch is a three-sentence narrative framework that, when done well, will help anyone—even people outside your industry—understand precisely the value you drive in your role, as well as the unique fullness of who you are. Even if you currently feel like a small fish in a big ocean, the fact that there is an existing role for your type of work experience proves there is a need for the responsibilities you manage. Instead of appearing meek or indecisive, you will come off as confident and prepared.

Additionally, your elevator pitch gives others a framework to talk about you. It's important, particularly for underrepresented professionals, to create a narrative and brand using your own words versus allowing others to share based on their perceptions and observations of you. No one can describe your value better than you, and therefore you should be the one driving that conversation.

Where and How to Use Your Elevator Pitch

Before we dive in and start writing, I want to share some scenarios where your elevator pitch will be useful.

Scenario #1

You're at a company event and have a chance to meet an executive you admire. This person is not usually accessible, so having face time with her is a rare opportunity. You want to foster rapport with her, with the goal of exploring mentorship or sponsorship. When she asks, "What do you do here?" what will you say?

Most individuals would answer that question in three parts: name, title, and department. For example, "I'm an accountant within the Marketing organization." But, by sharing your elevator pitch, you'll be able to communicate exactly how you drive impact for the overall business within your role.

Scenario #2

You get an interview for an exciting position at one of your dream companies. This role will allow you to leverage your greatest skills and strengths while giving you the new challenge and increase in seniority you're looking for. This type of position is rarely available, so you know you'll be competing with many internal employees as well as other top candidates. Your interview panel opens the conversation by asking, "Tell me about yourself." What will you say?

Again, most individuals will say something generic that does not add relevancy or context to their interest in the role, why they would be a good fit, or how the opportunity aligns to their passion. Instead, they'll say, "I'm originally from New York. I moved here three years ago for my current role as a Customer Relationship Manager. I saw the role you're offering and it looked incredibly exciting." By answering this way, they've missed the opportunity to make a lasting first impression, set the tone for the conversation, and stand out from other candidates. In this scenario, your elevator pitch will set you apart from the start.

Scenario #3

You're out for dinner one evening and strike up a conversation with someone at the bar. Turns out, she is an engineer who works for one of your top companies. You currently work in marketing in a non-technical field. When she asks, "What do you do?" how will you respond?

When you have your elevator pitch memorized, it can help you communicate your role and unique value even to people who have no understanding of your industry. An engineer may have no idea what a marketing role entails, but they probably know people in the marketing department of their company! In fact, they may be connected with someone who is hiring for a role you'd be perfect for. This is exactly what happened to me when I met Lisa at that birthday party.

***

As you think about your professional development and advancement as a whole, you will want to be ready for these scenarios (and countless others) when they arise. The elevator pitch framework you're about to learn has been tested across various professional environments, and it works.

THE ELEVATOR PITCH FRAMEWORK

I've condensed the often-complex process of writing your elevator pitch down to a simple, three-sentence format.

- *Sentence #1:* The headline of your current role and responsibilities, what you're measured on, and how you specifically help to drive value across your company.
- *Sentence #2:* The ways in which you drive impact *outside* of your direct role but still add value to your company. This could include volunteer work, mentorship, public speaking, leading groups within your organization, or taking on projects outside of the scope of your responsibilities.

- *Sentence #3:* What you are passionate about and enjoy outside of work. (Note: this sentence can and should be removed in certain professional environments. I'll explain why shortly.)

As you can see, it's fairly simple to create a powerful elevator pitch. However, it's not always easy, because that's a lot of information to cram into three sentences!

Let's look a bit deeper.

Sentence #1: The Headline of Your Current Role and Responsibilities

Creating a "headline" from your job title isn't as simple as plugging in your title and company name. It's about demonstrating specific competencies, responsibilities, and value metrics.

The best way to understand how to write an effective headline is by reading examples from others. While these examples might not resonate with you or be relevant to your line of work, pay attention to how these individuals have shifted the narrative from job title to headline.

> ***Title:*** Director of Ad Sales at LinkedIn
> ***Headline:*** "I'm a Director of Ad Sales at LinkedIn and lead a team of six Sales Managers who are responsible for helping LinkedIn's top clients advertise their businesses on the LinkedIn platform."

Through this explanation, I learned that this person is in a leadership role, that she manages a team of six people, and that she teaches clients how to effectively advertise their businesses on LinkedIn.

> ***Title:*** Executive Assistant at Visa.
> ***Headline:*** "I am the right hand to the Chief Diversity Officer at Visa and oversee various business priorities to make Visa a more diverse, equitable, and inclusive workplace."

An executive assistant can wear many hats, so this person has simplified their role description and instead leaned into the benefit they bring to the workplace. See how they pivoted the perception of administrative duties to being a key driver toward corporate values?

> ***Title:*** Production Engineer
> ***Headline:*** "As a Production Engineer, I design and develop chips and applications that power Toyota cars."

This description moved us away from a vague title and toward an understanding of the importance of this person's work to the overall success of the company and its customers.

***

How much more did you learn about the above professionals through their headlines than you would have through their job titles alone? How could knowing the full scope of your role help others understand the tremendous value you drive for your teams, your customers, your organization, and your company as a whole?

Write Your Own Sentence #1

We're going to take this piece by piece. I'll guide you along the way to make this a seamless experience. The headline is the most complex of the three sentences in your elevator pitch, but with a bit of brainstorming and some iteration, you'll land on a headline that conveys what you do with clarity.

So, download the Elevator Pitch Template at www.devikabrij.com/thriveincolor (or grab your paper journal) and write down the following:

1). Your job title.

2). The name of the company you work at.

3). Who you are responsible for partnering with in your role. (For example, if you're in sales or customer service, you likely work with customers. If you work in corporate communications, HR, or are a people manager, you work with the company's employees. If you're in product management, you work cross-functionally across many different groups internally, including the engineering and marketing teams.)

4). Write down three to five bullet points about what you're responsible for in your role today. Think about where you're measured or evaluated by your managers. A good practice here is to pull the job description of the role you're in today and see how your company communicated the responsibilities of your current role when they hired you.

5). Write down action verbs that best describe what you do day-to-day. For example: teach, coach, manage, promote, recruit, identify, build, develop, drive sales, strategize, etc.).

After you've completed this brainstorm, take all of the inputs above and combine them to create one sentence that includes all of them. Below is an example of how that might look for a Director of Sales at Company XYZ:

1). Director of Sales

2). Company XYZ

3). She is responsible for supporting and working with her clients who are Fortune 500 companies.

4). She is mainly responsible for educating her clients on Company XYZ's advertising solutions, and teaches Fortune 500 companies how to promote their brands and drive sales on the Company XYZ platform.

5). Action verbs she uses to describe her sales role are "teach," "promote," and "drive sales."

So, using all of these inputs from her brainstorm, this person's one-sentence headline is:

"As a Director of Sales at Company XYZ, I teach my clients who are Fortune 500 companies how to successfully promote their brands and drive sales of their products on the Company XYZ platform."

See how clearly and succinctly she explained the core of her role and responsibilities? Anyone—even those who might not have experience with sales, marketing, or advertising roles—will understand exactly what she does after just one sentence.

Sentence #2: The Ways in Which You Drive Impact *Outside* of Your Direct Role but Still Add Value to Your Company

Now that you have completed your headline, let's move on to the second sentence of your elevator pitch.

Sentence #2 is just as important as Sentence #1. It communicates how you are driving impact outside the core responsibilities of your role. These are areas that you're passionate about and that create impact for your company, team, clients, and community, even though you are not directly responsible for or measured on them in your primary role.

These areas can include but are not limited to coordinating and managing off-site team-building events, mentoring your peers, volunteering within your company's employee resource groups, serving on boards or committees, or sharing industry insights on panels, podcasts, or other channels.

For this sentence, identify and write down your interests and/or the ways you're driving impact. Then, construct Sentence #2 from the information you've brainstormed. To make this easier, try starting with the words, "I'm also committed to …" and then complete the sentence using the areas you identified.

For example, the Director of Sales at Company XYZ enjoys elevating her peers by mentoring them and volunteering within the Black Employee Resource Group. So, her Sentence #2 might be, "I'm also committed to elevating my peers through mentorship and volunteering with the Black employee resource group."

Don't be afraid to share here. What seems mundane or unimportant to you could be the reason you get that next opportunity!

Sentence #3: What You Are Passionate About and Enjoy Outside of Work

For most people, Sentence #3 is the easiest one to create. It's communicating what you enjoy doing in your personal life, outside of work, and speaks authentically to you as a whole being. For me, and for so many underrepresented individuals I've worked with, highlighting areas in our personal life that matter to us helps to minimize imposture syndrome. It allows us to shed light on the areas that feel most authentic and enjoyable to us—our most human sides.

To construct Sentence #3, write down a few things you enjoy doing outside of work. These might include (but certainly aren't limited to):

- Family and children
- Travel
- Volunteer or charity work
- Sports
- Hobbies
- Playing an instrument
- Singing in a choir
- Podcasting
- Creative or professional writing

When you've gathered your list of passions and pursuits, choose two that you feel speak most clearly to the essence of who you are. Then, write your Sentence #3, starting with, "Outside of work,

I enjoy …" For example, the Director of Sales at Company XYZ plays soccer on a co-ed team and spends her free time mentoring at-risk youth. So, her Sentence #3 might be, "Outside of work, I play soccer with a co-ed team and serve as a mentor for at-risk youth."

Putting It All Together

Now for the fun part!

You've done the hard work of thoughtfully communicating your expertise and values by drafting your three sentences. Now, go ahead and combine them into a single paragraph.

To continue our example of the Director of Sales, her elevator pitch sounds like this:

> *"As a Director of Sales at Company XYZ, I teach my clients who are Fortune 500 companies how to successfully promote their brands and drive sales of their products on the Company XYZ platform. I'm also committed to elevating my peers through mentorship and volunteering with the Black employee resource group. Outside of work, I play soccer with a co-ed team and serve as a mentor for at-risk youth."*

Simple, right? Congratulations! You just created your very own, thoughtful, authentic, and concise elevator pitch!

Your next step is to memorize your elevator pitch so you have a response ready for when people inquire about you and your work in various professional environments.

I encourage you to look over your elevator pitch a few times after you complete it. Even better, read it aloud. You may decide to switch around some words or examples until you feel confident communicating your pitch from start to finish.

Once you've created your elevator pitch, it will be easy to update a few times a year as you evolve in your personal and professional life. Whenever you start a new job, take on a new role, or set a new career goal, you will want to change your elevator pitch to reflect that. At the very least, revisit your pitch every six months.

As I hinted earlier, it's also important to have different versions of your elevator pitch. In certain environments, communicating all three sentences of your elevator pitch is perfect, while in other situations, it may feel a bit random or awkward to include your personal interests. For example, if you're at a networking event and someone asks the classic question, "What do you do?" it may feel more natural to use the first two sentences of your elevator pitch that explain who you are professionally. If the person you're speaking with asks what you enjoy outside of work, Sentence #3 is there for you.

On the other hand, the third sentence is great because it helps people understand who you are, and not just what you do. When you're interviewing for a job or meeting a leader, sponsor, or mentor for the first time, Sentence #3 helps them get to know you and may help them feel more connected to you.

My suggestion is to memorize your entire elevator pitch and then use your discretion as to when to share or leave out Sentence #3.

Despite the brevity of your elevator pitch, these three sentences convey so much more about you than you can imagine. And so, I'll end this chapter by sharing my own elevator pitch.

> *As the CEO of Brij the Gap Consulting, I partner with corporations to develop and increase retention of their underrepresented and leaders. I'm also the Co-Founder of Zaka,*

a career development platform for immigrant professionals. Outside of my work, which is focused on elevating the careers of underrepresented professionals, I enjoy being active and traveling to new destinations.

Through my elevator pitch, you learned that I understand business strategy as a business owner, and that I create and teach strategies and frameworks that help underrepresented employees and senior leaders become better professionals. You also learned that I'm invested in underrepresented groups, especially ethnically diverse professionals.

Isn't that so much more memorable and authentic than, "Hi, I'm Devika, and I'm a consultant"?

Chapter Seven

YOUR EXECUTIVE SUMMARY

IN ONE OF MY previous roles at a major company, we experienced a re-org of our department.

This was common at this company; in fact, it happened on an annual basis. The shifts were typically positive, but this particular time, it was brutal. The company had acquired a marketing automation company with the intention of adding that company's product to its own marketing solutions offer suite. Shortly after the acquisition, our department had to restructure the account management teams. For me, this meant a shift from working with a supportive and hands-on manager who encouraged us to consistently highlight our contributions to the team to working with a new manager from the other company who had stayed through the acquisition. I'll call this new manager "Dara."

Dara was nice. She seemed excited to be with a bigger, globally known company, and I could tell she was eager to prove herself.

In her new role, she would be responsible for managing some employees in the United States as well as our team of five in Canada.

Given how close and tight-knit our team was, we all desired to build a relationship with her, but it quickly became apparent that Dara's priorities lay with the American team and not us. She hardly traveled to Canada to see us, rarely gave us opportunities to get face time with her in the New York office, and routinely canceled meetings and off-sites for our team. As they say, the writing was in the sand. She was managing us because she had to, but because Canada was a less "visible" market than her other direct reports managed, she didn't give us anything but the bare minimum. Dara was our manager on paper, but the rapport and relationship was nonexistent.

Imagine having to go through self-assessments and performance evaluations two or three times a year with a leader who has minimal investment in or clarity about your work and challenges. When my evaluation period arrived, I attached my executive summary into the company's portal to record self-assessment feedback, peer feedback, and manager feedback. I highlighted my contributions and wins in leadership, scaling solutions to business challenges, and results in the hope that these examples would showcase my achievements despite Dara's lack of involvement.

I was wrong. Dara completely disregarded both my executive summary and my self-assessment. Instead, she centered her feedback on areas she believed I could improve. Hardly anything she said encouraged the good work I was doing. It was all just criticism.

Perhaps I could have swallowed disappointment and acted on her areas of improvement if Dara had actually had any knowledge of or involvement in my career, but she was so removed that her feedback was not only irrelevant but blatantly incorrect. Still, I continued to update and share my executive summary. Most of the time, Dara wouldn't even acknowledge my emails updating her on my quarterly wins.

Luckily for my team and me, Dara was our manager for only one year. When it was time to meet with our new manager, Teri, she asked all the right questions to understand where I wanted to go within the company and how she could support me. I sent Teri the three executive summaries I had shared with Dara the year before, as context into how I was working to get to where I desired to be.

Teri was blown away. "Wow! This is so helpful for me to get acquainted with you and know how to support you! Can you share this with the wider team?"

I was so happy that I didn't let Dara's bad leadership interrupt the way I tracked and communicated my accomplishments. If I had stopped preparing and sharing my executive summaries, I would have had to build my reputation and rapport with Tara from scratch, which would have been incredibly frustrating and defeating given the year we'd just had. And, even better, Teri was able to help me get promoted later that year, in part by using my executive summaries as a tool to share my accomplishments with other decision-makers.

HOW DO YOU SUMMARIZE YOUR SUCCESS?

Now that you have mastered your verbal narrative (aka, your elevator pitch), it's time to move to your visual narrative, which is your executive summary.

An executive summary is a simple and easily digestible document that summarizes your key accomplishments, your career highlights, and how you drive value within the categories that best resonate with decision-makers. Those categories belong to the LSR Method I introduced in Chapter Four: leadership skills, scaling solutions, and results.

There are three major reasons to create an executive summary to support your career conversations:

1). To have an at-a-glance portfolio of your successes and the value you are driving for the company, your team, your peers, and your clients. This helps your leaders, mentors, and sponsors easily understand what you're doing and why it matters.

2). To communicate your contributions in a theme-based approach versus a list of random projects or initiatives. With this approach, your career narrative becomes strong, intentional, and rooted, making it much more memorable and usable for those who want to support and advocate for you.

3). To effectively track and reinforce examples of the great work you've done, and to record your contributions during each month, quarter, and year. This record of your successes continuously drives momentum for career conversations. Instead of plugging in your self-assessment via your company's internal tools, your executive summary will provide clear and concise examples of your great work. This makes it easy for decision-makers who have a say in your advancement but may not have much insight into your work to understand the value you bring and how you might contribute in a higher-level role.

All of these benefits are critical for underrepresented professionals who struggle with self-advocacy. If you feel uncomfortable making requests, sharing your career desires consistently, or straight up don't know how to approach elevating your work, you will want to spend the time to craft your executive summary.

Data is necessary for making decisions across every business, especially decisions around budget, payroll, and which resources require more investment for the business to succeed. When your leaders evaluate what you bring to the table, they are looking at these key areas. If they are going to invest more in you—whether that's through promotion, increased salary, additional training, or other development opportunities—they need to understand the data around your work and contribution.

The thing is, that data can only come from you. Nobody knows and can speak to your work better than you.

Proactively elevating your accomplishments may make you feel self-conscious, anxious, or even paralyzed because you're afraid to come across like you're bragging. I'll tell you this right now: *you're not bragging.* There is a clear distinction between a strong performer who is building their brand and sharing statistics about why their presence in the company contributes to success and someone who arrogantly takes credit for work that was a team effort or singles themselves out as the greatest thing since sliced bread.

As someone who has managed teams, I can tell you that when you share about your work, successes, and even areas of need, you make the role of your manager much easier. It takes the guesswork out of knowing what matters to you.

The key to successfully leveraging your executive summary (or any method of self-advocacy) is to practice healthy entitlement—aka, the "humble brag" which showcases your contributions through leading with data. The executive summary captures and presents this data in a way that is clear, concise, and can be easily circulated among multiple decision-makers. This is true whether you're sharing it internally in your company, in job interviews, or with mentors who do not work within your company.

Now, I won't lie to you: sometimes owning your narrative through an executive summary isn't well-received. It might be ignored (as mine was by Dara), or you may have a manager who actually pushes back when they receive this information. There are a variety of reasons for this. They could feel threatened by you. They may not believe that you are a strong performer, and your data discredits their beliefs. Or, it could be that they, too, struggle with self-advocacy, and therefore cannot receive someone who is advocating for themselves effectively, especially a person of color.

As I've mentioned in previous chapters, there are many things outside of your control, including the type of manager you have, but my call to action for you is to advocate for yourself anyway. If you will not advocate for yourself, who will? I can confidently say that, more often than not, the executive summary will be viewed as impressive by most of the people with whom you share it, and that good leaders will appreciate the intention and care it takes to create and present it. You cannot shrink yourself because your manager in this season of your career cannot receive your confidence and professionalism.

Before we dive into the instructions for creating your executive summary, I want to be real with you for a moment. Tackling this task will be challenging. In fact, it may be the hardest framework you will complete in this book. Why? First, because taking ownership of our value is hard, especially when, as underrepresented professionals, we've been minimized and put down for so long. Second, because it's tempting to think of our value in a task-based way, rather than a theme-based way, and you will have to step outside your comfort zone to do this well.

That said, this work is highly rewarding, and has been one of the biggest game-changers for my clients who have leveraged it.

A bonus benefit of this framework is that it's unique to Brij the Gap Consulting, so unless your leaders have engaged with someone who has gone through my training, they are unlikely to have seen a summary in this format. This will give you a competitive edge and help you appear (and feel) more prepared and intentional than others in your workplace. So please, stick with me, and give this your all. I'll guide you through every step and challenge and support you to think strategically about how you can convey your value in the most authentic way possible.

If you were hoping this chapter would be a passive read, I'm afraid it's not that kind of party. Creating your executive summary will take energy, curiosity, and the willingness to get uncomfortable. If that's not how you're feeling, I suggest taking a beat for yourself and coming back to this chapter when you're mentally prepared to build your game-changing narrative.

If you're ready now, let's do this!

THE BRIJ THE GAP EXECUTIVE SUMMARY FRAMEWORK

To recap, your executive summary is a short document that summarizes your key accomplishments, career highlights, and values within the skill categories that matter most to decision-makers: leadership, scaling solutions to business challenges, and results (LSR). The executive summary showcases your value in your own words, provides context for important career conversations, and highlights strengths and skills that may be missed in the wordiness of a typical resume. It ties together your accomplishments in a themed manner and helps you stand out from your peers in any conversation or interview. The information you include in your executive summary can capture your contributions throughout the course of your career (like a concise work portfolio), or focus on results you produced in a specific time frame (one particular quarter, the past six months, the past year, your entire time at that company, etc.).

Let's dive in.

Evidence Matters

No matter what industry, role, seniority level, or geographical location you currently occupy, the decision-makers and leaders who are evaluating you are looking for your leadership skills, your ability to create solutions to business challenges, and examples of your direct results. So, let's break down those three factors in the LSR Method.

- *Leadership* is about stepping up and taking ownership, helping clients and colleagues, mentoring, managing people, managing projects, volunteering, etc.
- *Scaling solutions* is about solving challenges for business needs and for your team, improving processes, and expanding solutions. You are doing this every day, whether you realize it or not!
- *Results* are about the direct impact of your work on team, company, and client outcomes. When we highlight direct impact through your results, it's communicating key facts, data, feedback or testimonials, awards, and other verifiable metrics and accolades.

I'm sure you're curious to know what an executive summary looks like. I won't keep you in suspense: here it is!

YOUR NAME
Executive Summary

Proven ability to ______________________________
and ____________________________________

Leadership

- Impact sentence #1
- Impact sentence #2
- Impact sentence #3

Scaling Solutions

- Impact sentence #1
- Impact sentence #2
- Impact sentence #3

Results

- Impact sentence #1
- Impact sentence #2
- Impact sentence #3

You can see that it's simple, with no graphics or busy designs. It's intentionally meant to look underwhelming to keep the attention on the examples you're including.

As you can see, your name is in a larger font than the rest of the document. This is intentional: it highlights your identity. Then, below, we have the headline, which is the one-liner of what you want to be known for, and which aligns with your self-created professional brand. Below that are three to five examples each of leadership, scaling solutions to business challenges, and results.

Yes, it really is that simple. But, as I've shared, creating it may not be easy. I know you're up for the challenge—so, download the Executive Summary worksheet at www.devikabrij.com/thrivein-color (or grab your paper notebook), complete the prompts in the upcoming sections, and begin building your executive summary.

Step 1: Identify Your Skills and Strengths

The first part is to make a list of skills and strengths you have self-identified through the CISS Framework in Chapter Four. If you haven't yet completed the CISS Framework, or if your skills and strengths still aren't clear to you, think about what skills you have been recognized for in the past, or that have been highlighted by co-workers, managers, mentors, sponsors, and clients as things you do particularly well.

As a refresher, some examples of skills might include:

- Problem-solving
- Data analysis
- Consulting
- Managing multiple projects
- Managing and leading team members
- Mentoring peers
- Fostering a collaborative culture
- Creating partnerships

- Creating strategies
- Making data-supported recommendations
- Client relationships and management

As you write down your skills, consider which "bucket" each skill falls into: leadership, scaling solutions, or results. Some skills might belong in multiple buckets, and that's okay; you can decide where they best fit later.

By the time you are done with this list, I want you to have at least three skills listed under each of the LSR buckets: three skills for leadership, three for scaling solutions, and three for results. These should also be relevant to your role and responsibilities and the skills you want to be known for.

Step 2: Identify Specific Scenarios

Now that you have three skills each for leadership, scaling solutions, and results, it's time to identify specific scenarios where you put each of those skills into practice and what the direct impact was for your team, your peers, your company, or your clients. These are called your "impact statements."

For example, say you listed "building and retaining teams" as a skill under leadership. An example of a time you put that skill into practice could be when you successfully built the marketing team with top talent and retained all employees this year by fostering a collaborative and trusting environment.

Or, if one of the skills you listed was "making data-supported recommendations," you could write about that time you used data to make strategic recommendations for savings during a key meeting, thereby helping the company save over $10,000 in the first quarter.

Try to include as many quantifiable examples as you can. If you have access to the data, cite it. However, if you do not have a line of sight into the end result of your contribution, that does not eliminate the work you did to get it there. There are thousands of ways to create correlations between your work and the outcomes it created. Just make sure your impact statements are relevant to not only what you do now, but also what you want to be known for.

There are thousands of ways to create correlations between your work and the outcomes it created. Just make sure your impact statements are relevant to not only what you do now, but also what you want to be known for.

To complete this step, write down impact statements for all of the nine (or more) skills you listed across the LSR buckets. Take your time with this. You will likely have many more examples to pull from than you realized!

Step 3: Transfer to Your Executive Summary Template

Hopefully, by this point, you're feeling motivated and confident. You now have evidence of the tremendous value you drive in critical areas that help your team and company thrive.

Now, transfer your impact statements to the executive summary template as your contributions under leadership, scaling solutions, and results. Again, there should be three examples (impact statements) under each category. Trust me when I say that this step is *so* satisfying!

Step 4: Build Your Headline

Your headline highlights your professional brand in a single powerful sentence. The headline goes at the top of the executive summary and leads your visual narrative, so it's important that it exemplifies the professional brand you are creating and want others to associate with you.

So, go back to the list of skills you refined earlier in this chapter. Read through them. Do you see any themes? Are there certain skills that you want to be associated with more than others? Do your skills show that you're meeting (or exceeding) the core responsibilities of your role? Are there skills that you are currently using that you'd like to employ more frequently? Are there skills you need to be known for to show you're a successful candidate for a promotion or new role?

After you've read through the list, choose the two skills that best represent your professional brand and what you want to be known for. For example, you might choose "Problem-solving/creativity" and "hiring and retaining talent" as your two top skills.

Then, create your headline by plugging the two skills you selected into this headline sentence:

"Proven ability to ________ and ________."

Since the two skills in my above example were "Problem-solving/creativity" and "hiring and retaining talent," the headline would read something like, "Proven ability to create effective solutions and successfully build and retain high-performing teams."

Now, it's your turn. Create your headline and paste it into your executive summary template.

LEVERAGING YOUR EXECUTIVE SUMMARY

Congratulations! You've completed all the parts of your executive summary. I know that was challenging. It's *supposed* to feel challenging. However, I promise you the hardest part is over. From here on out, every time you update your executive summary will be simpler.

I hope that, by leaning into this challenge, you have realized just how much value you actually are contributing within your current role. You are worthy of being acknowledged, supported, and rewarded for your work.

And that brings us to our next piece: leverage. Here are just a few ways you can leverage your executive summary and use it to build and reinforce your personal brand:

- Send your executive summary to HR or the interview panel before a job interview.
- Include it with your resume to provide more context or highlight areas you want to draw attention to. You will stand out in an interview process because hardly anyone uses an executive summary this way!
- Send it to your leaders ahead of performance reviews, evaluations, or any formal career conversation. (You could also attach it into the internal systems your company uses to capture your self-evaluations and performance reviews.)

- Use it to make a case for a promotion or salary increase. (In this case, you'd want to adapt the summary to include the impact you've had from the time you started in your role until the present day, to give it a wider lens.)
- Present it during informational interviews when meeting with leaders, decision-makers, potential mentors, or sponsors to give them context into who you are and why they should consider working with you. You will make a lasting impression by showing up prepared.

Another key piece of leverage: make sure that if someone is telling stories about you, it's because you told them those stories. *Never* let anyone else create your narrative and share it on your behalf. When you create a robust executive summary and pair it with your elevator pitch, you will have taken big strides toward owning your narrative. You are in the driver's seat in your career, and owning your narrative is a key piece of commanding the respect and attention of your audience. Whether you're looking for a new position, a promotion, or simply reinforcing your current personal brand, a strong executive summary will always be an effective framework to convey your value, strengths, and skills in a way that resonates with different employers and personalities and creates a case to receive what you want.

Chapter Eight

CULTIVATING YOUR NETWORK OF ADVOCATES

MY COLLEAGUE, ZAHRA, once lost out on a promotion that she was highly endorsed for and was working toward for months because of a referral from the head of the organization. The referral's father had been in the same fraternity as the head of the organization thirty years prior, and they were still friends.

Never have I seen an applicant get pushed through the system so fast. This young man was interviewed simply for optics and to ensure nobody caused a stink before being offered a salary well above the pay range. It all happened in the blink of an eye.

It didn't matter how deserving Zahra was, or how hard she'd worked to position herself for this role. In the end, this young man's access, gained through his father's network, gave him the upper hand over a worthy, hardworking internal employee. His performance over the eighteen months he spent in that role was underwhelming, yet his position was protected due to his relationship with leadership, and the other decision-makers he was now friendly with as a result of that relationship.

Zahra, on the other hand, left the company. Fortunately, she ended up landing a role with a better title and salary—but the company still lost out on a dedicated and talented underrepresented employee.

While I was working at the social media platform, my white female manager, Heather, who I shared about in Chapter Two, and our white female colleague, Shannon, bonded over material topics like designer clothing, exclusive restaurants, and luxury travel. Now, I like nice things, and I also like learning about the interests of others, but I didn't have much to contribute to their discussions. My weekends were mostly spent taking care of my aging grandmother, while theirs were spent at luxurious spas and trendy restaurants. Instead of opening our Monday morning meeting with, "How was your weekend?" or "What did you do on Saturday?" they would ask, "Did you hang out with your grandma again this weekend, Devika?" This would lead to me awkwardly waiting for them to stop gushing over their weekend in the Hamptons or the happy hour hosted by the head of our organization at his Silicon Valley home.

I want to be clear: there was nothing wrong with Heather and Shannon's choices, nor with mine. I had made a decision to take care of my grandmother; I wasn't resentful or disappointed that I was spending my weekends with her instead of accompanying my officemates on their adventures. I also love good wine and weekends in the Hamptons, but at that time in my life, I simply didn't share Shannon and Heather's experiences or priorities.

However, in this situation, my differing priorities did work against me. Shared interests often create bonds that, consciously or unconsciously, result in greater availability of access, resources, and opportunities to those in the "in-crowd," particularly with white males. The "boy's club" mentality is still alive and well.

Over time, I noticed that Shannon—in part because of her shared interests and seamless bond with Heather—always had a good experience getting her requests heard. On the other hand, I always had to create a case for what I was proposing. (As you'll remember from Chapter Two, this eventually escalated into friction over my hotel selection.) Would things have been different if I had been part of that weekend "in-crowd"? I don't know, but I think they might have.

Accessing and maintaining a network of advocates—mentors, sponsors, and supporters—has historically been challenging for professionals of color. All relationships are nuanced, and shared interests and experiences are only a part of the puzzle. But I can tell you that building authentic connection and cultivating a network of advocates can, if approached correctly, be one of the most rewarding parts of your career journey.

Perhaps you understand the benefits of having a network of advocates, but the thought of approaching a mentor or sponsor feels intimidating. If you've ever felt self-conscious or anxious asking someone for this kind of support, I assure you, you're not alone. Most people show up to such engagements lacking structure, and therefore also lacking expectation. As a result, the relationships tend to fizzle as fast as they started, leaving the person needing support feeling unworthy and deflated.

A challenge I hear often from clients is, "I have a great mentor, but I'm not really sure how to navigate that relationship." Or, they might say, "I have a sponsor who is willing to advocate for me, but I'm not sure how to leverage that person. This sponsor is committed and we're meeting regularly, but I'm not getting what I need."

Then, of course there's this one: "My company paired me with a mentor and it's a horrible match. How do I get out of this?"

A big challenge for underrepresented professionals is the discomfort they feel approaching leaders and colleagues for help in achieving growth opportunities. Some are fearful of rejection; some do not feel smart, worthy, or qualified enough. Some simply do not know how to approach or engage the individuals they'd like to partner with. These are very common challenges, and often cause people to avoid the question of finding mentors or sponsors altogether.

The good news is, it's not as hard as it seems. In this chapter, we'll learn not only how you can identify and approach aligned mentors, sponsors, and advocates, but also how to structure those relationships so both you and your advocates can get the most possible value from your time together.

RELATIONSHIPS MATTER

Relationships Matter. This is one of LinkedIn's core values, and the one I resonated most with during my time working there. These two words are also arguably the most important guidance I can give you with regard to your career.

Most professionals realize the power of good relationships in their immediate environment. For example, being on good terms with your team is helpful, since you likely need to cooperate with them to execute your role. Similarly, it's obvious that a strong relationship with your direct manager is important because they play a significant role in both your daily work and your career trajectory. It's easy to put all your eggs in your direct manager's basket, highlighting your achievements and advocating for your needs with that one person.

But what happens if you don't feel comfortable with your manager? What if your manager brings their internal biases to bear when making decisions about your advancement, or is simply not as committed to your career growth as you are? What happens if a manager goes on a leave of absence, moves to another department, or leaves the company entirely? How would that impact your career goals and the momentum you've built?

If you want to take control of your career trajectory and own your narrative both within and outside the bubble of your team or department, it's essential to build authentic relationships with multiple individuals who genuinely desire to help you, advocate for you, and champion you for opportunities. I call this group of individuals your "network of advocates."

Notice that I said "authentic relationships." There has to be purpose, intention, and care behind the relationships you cultivate and nurture. If you pursue relationships from the perspective of, "How can this person help me get what I want?" it will be evident to the person being used for their access and resources; in such cases, not only will they be far less inclined to help you, but they will also let their own networks know about your transactional approach. So, instead of selfishly using people to climb the ladder of your career, treat the members of your personal network of advocates like a valued part of your team. They should know that you specifically chose to partner with them and understand the reasons behind your decision. More, you should be clear about what you bring to the relationship so that it feels mutually beneficial.

Having a network of advocates is especially important for historically marginalized people who struggle with self-advocacy and experience systemic barriers in the workplace. Most of us don't have parents with old fraternity connections to CEOs or other established networks within the corporate world—but even if we do, our first instinct isn't to leverage them. It feels uncomfortable, and most of us feel we need to earn our place and prove our worth instead of expecting a leg up. We don't have an expectation that doors will open for us. We're more likely to have received advice like, "Don't share your career aspirations with anyone," or, "She's an executive. She's too busy to meet with you." This feedback is likely rooted in the experiences of our parents, family, and friends who were unfavorably compared to their peers, experienced overt racism in the workplace, dealt with jealous or competitive colleagues and managers, or were sabotaged by others in pursuit of opportunities. It's also likely reinforced by our own experiences in the workplace.

In every company and industry, there are individuals you can share with, trust, and collaborate with to help you move the needle in your career. They are the people you will focus on when building your personal network of advocates.

Why Do You Need Advocates?

I wish I had known the long-term impact and importance of having a personal network of advocates early in my career. It would have alleviated so much of the pressure I felt while trying to navigate challenges in the workplace. The truth was, I didn't have to do it alone. There were several influential leaders around me who would have gladly stood in my corner if I hadn't allowed self-doubting thoughts like, "Why would they want to help?" to sabotage me, or pre-judged whether someone would be a good mentor or advocate for me without actively qualifying them.

I won't lie, it takes work and discernment to build and maintain your network of personal advocates, and it can feel daunting to begin if you don't have a clear grasp of the benefits. So, let's take a look at what a personal network of advocates can offer.

Among the many benefits of cultivating your personal network of advocates are:

- Access to opportunities
- Support in navigating challenges
- Building a professional network
- Increased confidence and motivation

Let's look at each of those in more depth.

Access to Opportunities

Access to opportunities in the workplace is not always equitable. Having individuals in your corner who hold influential positions can open doors to high-visibility work and projects, promotions, and leadership positions that might otherwise be difficult to attain.

Support in Navigating Challenges

In addition to the usual challenges that everyone faces in their careers, as underrepresented professionals we also deal with explicit and implicit bias, institutionalized discrimination, and other sets of challenges. Having a support system of people who have experienced similar challenges and understand the nuances of navigating these environments can offer valuable insight, guidance, and emotional support.

Building a Professional Network

Access to a broader network can open doors to new career opportunities and mentorship from other influential and experienced professionals. As we've explored, many underrepresented professionals do not have access to these individuals through their immediate personal networks. Therefore, we have to build them—and connecting with mentors, sponsors, and other advocates is a powerful way to accomplish this.

Increased Confidence and Motivation

The right group of advocates can boost your confidence and help you overcome imposter syndrome and self-doubt. This, in turn, helps you become a more effective self-advocate and to be more assertive when articulating your value and making an ask. Additionally, having a network of advocates who are people of color themselves can be incredibly empowering. Seeing individuals who look like you achieve success in senior and executive positions will inspire you to set ambitious career goals for yourself.

***

The support, guidance, and access your personal network of advocates can provide will have long-term effects on your career trajectory and overall career satisfaction.

Many of the organizations I partner with offer wonderful mentorship and sponsorship programs for their employees. In fact, you may already be a part of a similar internal program that has matched you with a mentor. However, my feedback to leaders—and now, to you—is that it cannot be assumed that employees know how to best engage in a relationship with their assigned mentor or sponsor. This unique dynamic is not something that most marginalized individuals (like people of color, immigrants, and women) have been proactively taught. The result is that underrepresented professionals and women will encounter struggles while building new relationships and networks that white, cisgender men do not experience.

Why does this happen? There are several reasons, but here are three that I think are relevant to our conversation here.

First, most networking happens during social gatherings, informal meetings, or after-work events. White males have been historically overrepresented in positions of influence, leading to a dominant presence in networking circles; this makes it easier for them to connect and build relationships with others who share similar backgrounds and experiences. People of color often find themselves in smaller numbers within these circles, making it harder to find relatable peers and leaders to network with, which can lead to reluctance to engage.

Most of my clients and the people of color in my network despise after-work events because they feel so forced. If you don't go, you are likely to be branded "disengaged" or not a team player. If you force yourself to go, you will expend a large amount of mental and emotional energy for what can feel like very little gain. Yes, networking events can be fun and rewarding, especially if you enjoy your teammates and company culture, but if you feel forced to attend or simply don't enjoy socializing outside of work, it can feel daunting.

Second, people of color and women often have different dynamics outside of work to contend with than their white male peers. While my colleagues were touring wineries on the weekends, I was caring for my grandmother. Again, there was nothing wrong with this—it was a choice I was glad to make—but it did impact my ability to connect with my teammates and manager. People of color, especially women of color, often have greater responsibilities in their home lives that preclude extracurricular activities like networking, happy hours, or weekend travel with colleagues. More, we often have cultural expectations around family and caregiving that differ from those of our white peers. While these dynamics are shifting as gender roles and societal norms become more fluid, they are still very much present and need to be considered.

Finally, while shared experiences and networks are often enough for white professionals, especially white, cisgender men, to connect and access opportunities and introductions to influential people, people of color and women often face the additional hurdle of needing to prove their value before those same doors are opened for them. This requires us to have a plan for approaching people of influence with greater structure, planning, and formality. Once you have built your personal network of advocates, however, this dynamic can be lessened greatly.

WHO ARE YOUR ADVOCATES?

So, who belongs in your personal network of advocates?

There are three groups of individuals who will form the foundation of your network. In this section, we'll look at who these people are, how they differ, and how to build and maintain momentum in your engagements with them.

Mentors

Mentors are experienced and trusted advisors who guide, support, offer advice, and share their own experiences with you to make you a better professional. These are typically people who have cultivated a specific area of expertise, and who, as a result, can support you with career planning, skill development, navigating challenges in the workplace, and making informed decisions. Moreover, they are people you respect, admire, and are excited to learn from.

Mentors are typically more experienced than you but have overcome similar obstacles and walked in your shoes at some point in their career. Maybe they're in the role you're currently trying to move into, or maybe they have been in the role you're in today. They can also be your peers—even if they're not senior to you—if they have the knowledge and perspective you need to advance in this season of your career.

Mentorship can be a formal arrangement through workplace mentoring programs, educational institutions, or introductions through your network. Or, it can be an informal connection that develops naturally between two individuals. Overall, think of mentors as those who guide, teach, and support you through your career trajectory and help you become the professional you want to evolve into by investing their expertise and knowledge in you.

I am often asked, "Is it better for me to have a mentor inside the company I work for, or outside?" The answer is, look for both! It's of benefit when mentors work in your company because they are familiar with the company culture, policies, politics, leaders, and other relevant information that could help you; however, if they do not work at your company, they can offer an outsider's perspective which can be incredibly helpful. In my own career, I chose to have mentors both within and outside of the company I was working at, and that variety proved to be highly effective.

Sometimes, your greatest mentors will be people you will never meet. Yes, you read that right. Your mentors can be industry leaders, pastors, coaches, and other people who inspire you through podcasts, books, social media, courses, and other indirect methods. I call these people "distant mentors." Distant mentors have created massive impacts in my own career journey. I may not have had face-to-face interactions with them, and to this day many of them still have no clue who I am, but I still received significant guidance from the information they shared through their platforms.

Now, let's talk about who mentors are *not.*

A mentor is not a cure for low self-esteem or someone whose job it is to make you feel validated. If you are feeling consistently down or lacking confidence, my suggestion is to seek counseling or therapy (which I believe every individual on this planet needs). Think of it this way: it's the job of a therapist to help you process, but it's the job of a mentor to help you move forward. It is not your mentor's responsibility to make your hard problems go away, or to be a sounding board for personal or inter-office dramas. Of course, if you're having a bad day or struggling with a particular situation, it's perfectly fine to bring this to your mentor and receive feedback, but if negative feelings or emotional crises are happening consistently, a counselor or therapist will serve you better.

Sponsors

The second category in your personal network of advocates—and, in my opinion, the most important—are sponsors.

Sponsors are influential decision-makers, typically senior-level leaders, who agree to support your professional development and advancement by advocating for you. A sponsor uses their access, influence, networks, and relationships with other leaders and decision-makers to champion your work and position you for opportunities, while removing any barriers you may experience as an underrepresented professional. Sponsors ensure you are considered for promotion and rewards, high-visibility projects, and other opportunities that benefit your career trajectory and growth. Unless you are planning to make a move to a new company, your sponsors will typically come from inside your organization.

Sponsors can also provide mentorship in your relationship, and having a person who acts as both sponsor and mentor can help you keep your network of advocates lean, and your time commitments more streamlined. Like mentors, they may organically provide transparent advice and feedback as you discuss your career—but that is not their main function. Their job is to take an active role in increasing your visibility for career growth within your company, which means they hold a responsibility to highlight and champion you that mentors do not.

In my opinion, having a sponsor at every stage of your career is critical, especially as a person of color, and especially if you struggle with self-advocacy. However, sponsors are only beneficial when you are prepared to leverage them. Keeping in mind that your sponsors are there to elevate your professional brand and build your credibility and reputation across the company, you can provide them with powerful information to use and share on your behalf. And (if you haven't already guessed), the best way to do this is by utilizing the tools we've already covered in this book: your CISS Framework, elevator pitch, and executive summary.

Remember, you need to lead the narrative you want leaders and influential people to share on your behalf. Sponsors need to understand what you want to be known for so they can help increase your visibility. Even the best, most hands-on sponsors won't know how to drive impact for you unless you inform them of your goals and specific ideas you have on how they can help you meet them. They will be willing and excited to help, but it's your responsibility to drive the narrative and make it easy and rewarding for them to help you.

If you're thinking, "But Devika, I don't know what I want to do. I'm still figuring that out!" I totally get it, and it's okay to not have a complete picture of where you want to be in five years, or ten. However, you need to have some ideas and options framed out if you're going to approach a sponsor for help. For example, you might not know the exact role you want to pursue, but you might have an idea about the type of work you want to do, the skills you want to learn, or the seniority level you want to achieve. Sharing this with your sponsor will allow them to help you fill in the blanks and identify the most powerful next steps. That said, if you're in a season of feeling lost or unclear about your entire career direction, it would serve you well to lean into a mentor who can help you explore your options while you work with your sponsor to highlight the great work you're doing in your career right now. This reinforces your brand and the good work you're doing, so when you do get clarity on your next steps, you're ready to leverage everything you've been accomplishing in the meantime.

Career Allies

The current definition of an "ally" in the social sphere is someone who is not a member of an underrepresented group but who takes action to support that group. However, in this context, think of a career ally as being similar to a sponsor but without the need to be more senior than you.

Have you ever considered leveraging your peers or even those junior to you for your career advancement? These individuals are often overlooked, but in most cases, they have the most visibility into your work, your success, your value, and even the challenges you face in the scope of your role. They see you navigating the day-to-day. Think of the peers on your team, particularly those who have the ear of a decision-maker you wish to influence. You can also create an allyship with a cross-functional partner who is not part of your direct team but with whom you collaborate often.

Not every peer can be a great career ally. Your career allies need to be people you trust and can be honest with about your career advancement desires. They need to genuinely support you and believe in your potential for advancement, as well as be people you genuinely connect with on a personal level. Think about who you would willingly have lunch, dinner, or drinks with outside of work, and who you can be vulnerable and transparent with when you're having a tough day or navigating a challenge.

If you don't have such relationships currently, please don't force it. If you don't have trusting relationships with your team members—for *any* reason—you should not approach them to be your career allies. Career allies have a shared trust and a mutual desire to see each other win, and as such do not engage in competition or feel threatened by one another. It's a relationship that should be approached delicately. You want a career ally who will have your back even if you are promoted over them—and who, in turn, you will still be able to rely on if they are promoted over you.

CULTIVATING PURPOSEFUL RELATIONSHIPS

When engaging mentors, sponsors, or career allies, it's vital to clearly communicate the nature of the relationship you wish to have with them, as well as the reasons you have chosen them as a partner in your career.

Title and seniority level are not enough to create a real relationship. It's about finding a good match for you. So, when you identify someone as a possible mentor, sponsor, or career ally, consider what about this person draws you to them beyond their current role. Maybe it's their empathetic leadership approach, or the fact that they have held one or more roles that you would like to achieve. Maybe you're from similar ethnic, national, or cultural backgrounds, or grew up in the same city. Think about what that something special about this individual is, and communicate it.

Then, confirm exactly what you need from and are asking for from your potential mentor, sponsor, or career ally. Specifically, be clear about the time commitment you need from them and what support and connections you are hoping they will provide. Most people in a position to mentor or sponsor you are very busy, so if you approach them without a clear and direct ask, they may assume the partnership will be a heavier lift than what you're actually requesting and decline to partner with you. (And you know you'll be in your feelings if this happens.) So, enter into your initial conversations prepared to share precisely why you want their help, how you are imagining the relationship will work, and the time commitment you're asking for, so they can make an informed decision about supporting and advocating for you.

Just like your advocates don't want to waste their time helping someone who isn't clear, you don't want to waste your time on empty promises or advocates who don't follow through. Both situations can create the "3D" feelings (discontentment, defeat and doubt) we talked about in earlier chapters. So, be prepared to vet your potential advocates carefully. I'll show you how in the next section.

Qualifying Your Personal Network of Advocates

In this section, I'll give you an action plan to qualify, engage, and secure mentors and sponsors that will position you in a way that will elevate you beyond what you could accomplish on your own. These points are critical when selecting advocates, yet are not often talked about in conversations about mentorship and sponsorship.

Know What You're Really Seeking

Sometimes, we think we need someone to learn from or someone to champion us, but what we're really seeking is someone to care about us, to see us, and to hear us. In such cases, we are looking for *affirmation.* There's nothing wrong with wanting to be affirmed in your skills, talents, and career desires, but your personal network of advocates is not designed to fulfill that need. Instead, consider seeking therapy or coaching outside of your professional network to work on addressing that need.

Trust Your Gut

Relationships with mentors, sponsors, and career allies can have their own challenges. These people, while they are possibly more advanced in their careers than you are, are still humans with their own strengths, faults, flaws, and preferences. Therefore, it's important to use your wisdom and discernment when selecting potential advocates. Someone can look great on paper and care deeply about helping others but still not be the right fit to be an advocate for you.

Here's a great example. When I was building Brij the Gap, I had no blueprint for how to start a learning and development consulting firm and make it successful. I was put in touch with an individual who I thought could be a good mentor to me and help me create this next iteration of my career.

In our very first meet-and-greet, she leaned in and, with a look of care in her eyes, said, "Devika, I'm going to tell you the truth because I want you to succeed and be prepared for that success. It will likely take *ten years* to get your business off the ground. It's unrealistic to think that you will have a thriving business within a few years of starting. Also, you will need to figure out how to get followers on your social channels before people will take you seriously."

To be clear, I did not sense an ounce of malicious intent when she gave me her perspective. This was her personal belief and was likely tied to her own experience of starting a business. I thanked her for her advice and left the meeting feeling a bit defeated but also determined to beat the odds she'd laid out for me.

It would have been easy for me to accept her advice as truth. She was successful and had been in my shoes before. Her advice also fit the narrative I'd heard from other first-time entrepreneurs. However, in my heart, I knew that would not be my story. And so, I couldn't allow her words to penetrate my mind, my spirit, or my expectations. No matter how successful she was today, having her as my mentor would require me to spend valuable time and energy *unlearning* the feedback and advice she was giving me before I could build what I knew I was called to do. Knowing that the process of unlearning is actually much more difficult than learning something for the first time, I chose not to accept her offer of mentorship. Her advice was relevant to her own business, but it wasn't relevant to mine.

Within a year of starting my company, Brij the Gap, I secured several enterprise companies as clients and replaced my former corporate salary—all with only thirty followers on my Instagram page. I will always be grateful that I trusted my gut.

Mentors, sponsors, and career allies—and anyone else who provides you with advice and support—are humans, and even the most successful people have blind spots, biases, and limitations. That's why it's important to trust yourself and gut check each piece of advice, even when it's coming from someone you greatly respect and admire.

There is a fine line between receiving constructive criticism that supports your development and growth and allowing any perspective provided to you to become your reality. As you seek advice from people, be mindful of not hanging on to other people's perspectives that go against what you're truly capable of. Extract what is valuable, and use wisdom and discernment to toss out the rest. This will become easier with time as you build authentic relationships and figure out who is truly in your corner and leading with the best intentions for you.

Be Trustworthy

Just as you need to trust yourself and run every piece of advice through your own filters, you also need to be trustworthy to your network of advocates and fulfill your commitments to them.

Many of your mentors will have been in previous relationships with other mentees or people they've sponsored. It's possible that some of these people did not fulfill their part of the bargain. Perhaps they didn't keep confidentiality in the relationship, wasted the advocate's time and energy by not preparing for meetings, didn't implement the advice that was given, or failed to step up to meet the opportunities being offered. These situations happen more than you might think and can turn mentors and sponsors away from investing their time in mentees. For this reason, earning and keeping your mentor's or sponsor's trust is key. The strategies you're learning in this book will go a long way toward helping you scaffold your relationship and maintain that trust.

Minimize Competition

I've had colleagues I admired greatly and wanted to learn from, but at the end of the day, we were being considered for the same opportunities and promotions. Competition made our allyship and personal relationships more complex.

I believe you can still engage potential competitors as mentors, as long as you keep it real with both yourself (and them) and proceed with the understanding that you may eventually be competing with this person for the same opportunities.

It's tempting to perceive the word "competition" as negative, especially if you are an athlete or someone who participated in selective activities like drama, music, or debate. However, when it comes to your career, I'd like for you to think of a "competitor" as someone who has equal rights to opportunities and promotions in the workplace. As long as both parties can put the reality of these competitive opportunities in the corner, the relationship can remain authentic and trusting; however, if there is malicious intent or any feelings of threat, it's best to not engage this person as a potential advocate.

I was able to successfully engage my peers and direct team members as mentors and career allies because those individuals were not threatened by me, and I was not threatened by them. We each genuinely cared about each other and were cheerleaders for one another. When one of us received an opportunity or promotion, it was like a win for everyone. If that's not the vibe you're getting from your peers or leaders, it's best not to engage them for mentorship or advocacy. Rather, learn from them at a distance by observing how they operate and what makes them successful. Plenty can be gained simply by paying attention to talented individuals.

Release Your Expectations

A common limitation faced by professionals of color when selecting their personal network of advocates is an inflexible set of expectations about who these people are and what they should look like.

Diversity is vital to growth in nearly every situation, and your personal network of advocates is no different. Most people naturally gravitate toward those who look like them, talk like them, have similar personality traits to them, and share similar experiences. And, while having a mentor or advocate of a similar background to you can be incredibly beneficial given the commonalities of lived experience, race and gender do not need to be prerequisites for mentorship or sponsorship. In fact, by considering race or gender before actual skill sets, expertise, networks, and resources, you could be disqualifying advocates who could drive great value in your career.

My personal approach both as a leader and a person being mentored/sponsored has been to cultivate a diverse network that includes people of different races, genders, personalities, faith practices, life experiences, and communication styles. This helps me foster growth and avoid becoming stagnant.

LEVERAGING YOUR PERSONAL NETWORK OF ADVOCATES

In 2013, I moved from one large tech company to another. While this opportunity was exciting, it also required me to take a few steps back in my career in both the type of work I was doing and my salary. However, the steps back enabled me to gain experience and knowledge in a completely new field, and ultimately propelled me into a future I never imagined for myself.

I admit, at the time I received the offer, I had to battle with myself a bit. My ego said, "Devika, you're really taking a step back in your career after you just left one of the most well-known tech companies in the world? You're really willing to accept $20,000 less in salary?" But, when I quieted that voice inside of me and looked objectively at the choice I was making, I saw that, although this seemed like a step back on the surface, it was also giant steps forward.

This role would take me from a position that cast a wide net across several responsibilities to a position where I could become a subject matter expert in sales and advertising. This role would enable me to partner closely with sales executives, learn the world of advertising, and push me in uncomfortable but beneficial ways. Unless I went back to school to get a degree in advertising and marketing, it was unrealistic for me to expect to be able to make a parallel move to a position in that environment, so when the opportunity was presented to me, I jumped at it. Sure, the salary and title were lower, but I made a commitment to use this as a stepping stone into a new career path. For the next year, I would give this role my all and try my hardest to gain the knowledge and expertise I needed in order to be promoted to more meaningful work. I was willing to put in the effort and time to prove myself while staying true to my ambitions and personal brand.

In order to meet my goals, I needed to not only excel in my new role, but also leverage my personal brand and lean into my network of advocates.

How I Leveraged My Network of Advocates

Step 1: Identify My New Mentor and Sponsor

The person I chose to be both my mentor and sponsor ended up being my manager, the person who hired me for the role. I chose her specifically because, before becoming a manager, she had previously been in the role I really wanted—a role that was the natural progression of the more junior position I just had taken. She already knew what it would take to be considered for a role like that, and what skills I'd need to develop to succeed in it—and, since she would ultimately decide if and when I would receive a promotion, she was the person to whom I most needed to prove myself. She also had direct relationships with the organization's Director and VP, who would sign off on my future promotion.

Choosing her as both my mentor and sponsor was ideal because she served both purposes effectively. Having only one relationship to cultivate also allowed me to put more time and energy into our relationship. As I've shared, a slimmer team of advocates is ideal.

Step 2: Identify My Career Allies

I chose career allies who were peers on my team, one level higher in seniority than I was. I worked very closely with them in supporting their clients and accounts. They were in the role I eventually wanted to be promoted into, and we all reported to the same manager (my mentor/sponsor). After I ramped up in my current role and felt like I had a good grasp of how to operate successfully and manage my responsibilities without help, I started to take on additional responsibilities to support my career allies, such as helping to prepare presentations for client meetings and covering for them when they were out of the office. Not only did this give me some experience of the role I was working toward being promoted into, but it also helped me be seen as a team player and showed my career allies examples that I could do the job well.

It's important to note that I only spent, on average, one to two hours a week doing this. I didn't compromise my responsibilities in my current role, nor did I take on so much work that I lost my work/life balance. Also, I was very transparent in telling them that I was working on developing the skills necessary to move into the Client Manager role (their current role) when an opportunity became available, and asked outright if they were willing to help me get there. Honesty, vulnerability, and high trust made it easy for them to say yes to my request.

Step 3: Ask for Examples

Next, I asked my career allies to email our manager examples of the impact I was driving. I was very clear on what I needed them to highlight. For example, when I helped them prepare for a client meeting, I would say, "Hey, Belle. Can you email Daniella and share how much time I saved you in preparing for this meeting and how my contribution impacted the meeting specifically? And are you able to cc me on the note so I can keep it in my portfolio to share during my performance review?" This took the guesswork out of it for my career allies and made it easy and quick for them to support me. Also, by asking to be cc'd, it ensured that my manager knew this feedback was being shared with me, so when I brought it up during later conversations, I could take full credit for the contributions and value I was generating.

Repetition and taking ownership of your good work through healthy entitlement is key. My ownership of my narrative and value showed my manager and other decision-makers that I was building the skills necessary to be successful in the role. It also highlighted that I was a hard worker, goal-oriented, and a team player, and that I didn't just expect the promotion but was willing to actively pursue and make a case for it. This gave me a leg up compared to my competition in the interview process when the position I wanted did open. I'm positive that there were great candidates with far more experience than me, but I had proven that I wanted the role and was willing to work for it well before it became available.

Step 4: Support My Mentor/Sponsor to Build a Case with Leadership

My manager took the feedback and the examples my career allies shared and was able to build a case for my promotion with the Director and VP, who at that point didn't know me well. If my manager didn't have several examples of how I was working toward the promotion, I'm confident that the Director and VP would have wanted someone more senior to take the position. But, because I diligently and indirectly created a portfolio of my work that highlighted my value, and had my career allies advocating for me, my manager had everything she needed to prove I was a great fit for the role.

Step 5: Ask My Allies to Advocate with the Hiring Manager

During the interview process, I asked my career allies to send emails to the hiring manager stating why I would be a great fit for the role. The hiring manager was able to forward these proactive recommendations to the executives who would ultimately sign off on my promotion.

***

Thanks to the strategic ways I created and leveraged my personal network of advocates, I ended up getting the role I wanted within just eleven months of joining the company, despite not having the tenure and expertise possessed by other candidates. This promotion also came with two times the salary I was making when I first joined the team in the more junior role—significantly more than my salary with my previous company. So, my "step back" in my career ended up being a giant step forward, thanks to the strategies you're about to learn in this chapter.

MAKE YOUR ADVOCATE RELATIONSHIPS SUCCESSFUL

Preparing for and maintaining your relationships with mentors, sponsors, and career allies takes strategy, just like I just shared with you in the previous section. Making these relationships successful and creating momentum is not as low-lift or passive as most people believe. However, the time and energy you spend in this sphere will be highly rewarding and will definitely move the needle in your career.

The way most work relationships operate is not optimal. It's fast-moving, unintentional, impersonal, and quite frankly, selfish. Most people approach relationships wanting to receive rather than to give—and the mentors and sponsors you may want to pursue are no different. Imagine being a leader (or someone who has a notable brand) and constantly being approached for help without any true intent, communication, or preparation. That would get old fast, right? You might even start to wonder, "What's in this for me?"

I want you to be seen in a different light. I want you to be prepared, intentional, empathetic, and highly professional, so that the people you ask to join your network of advocates are not just elevating you, but are also elevated by their association with you.

The strategy I'm about to share is broken into three parts: mentors, sponsors, and career allies. Each category of advocates requires a slightly different approach.

Identifying and Engaging the Right Mentors and Sponsors

Before you approach and engage mentors and sponsors, you first must gain clarity on why you selected that person and what you are asking from them. So, download the Mentor/Sponsor/Career Allies Worksheet template at www.devikabrij.com/thriveincolor (or your paper journal) and let's brainstorm together.

Mentors Brainstorm

To begin, write down your overall goal for engaging a mentor at this time. Essentially, I want you to identify what you need from a mentor by partnering with them. Your goal can be a promotion, moving into a higher seniority role, learning a new function, moving into a new industry, developing a specific skill set, or whatever else is top-of-mind for you. For example, if you want to transition from a sales role to a product role, your goal might be, "Learn about product to help me transition from sales into the product function." That's a great place from which to engage a mentor because it's specific and has clear outcomes.

Next, write down the exact areas you need help or insight in. Be as specific as possible. For example, you might want to learn about how a mentor managed their own career trajectory, expanded their own professional network, or navigated a specific industry. You might also want a mentor to offer feedback on your work, advocate for you for a promotion, champion you for open roles, or help you scale your brand with decision-makers. To continue the above example, the person who wants to move from sales to product might write the following as a goal: "Learn how a mentor ended up building a career in product, what she suggests I do to pivot from sales to products, and how she thinks I should approach conversations with decision-makers so they know my desire to switch to a different department but grow within the company."

Next, identify the time commitment you are asking for. In my experience, most mentors will happily agree to support you if your ask is feasible. So, use your judgment about how often you really need to meet with this person. If you expect your engagements to be more conversational and not urgent, a thirty-minute meeting per month, or even per quarter, is a great place to start. For executives and higher-ups in large companies who travel frequently and rarely have free time in their calendars, thirty minutes every six months might be the way to go. If your need is urgent—for example, if you're actively interviewing for a role or have a promotion opportunity that is fairly immediate—asking for thirty minutes twice a month for a short period of time is fair, as long as there is an end date attached.

The next step in your mentor brainstorm is one that often gets left out of the discussion—and that is to name the characteristics you need and want your mentor to have. Why is this important? It's critical to know the type of person you want to partner with in this season of your career. Do you want them to be patient, or direct and blunt? Do you want them to push you beyond your comfort zone, or be more nurturing? Do you want them to make you feel empowered where you are, or to challenge you to move beyond your comfort zone? For example, the person moving from sales to product may desire someone who is honest, nurturing, trustworthy, collaborative, and supportive, since they are likely to stumble a bit as they enter a brand-new space, and will fare better with someone who can help them remember that they're doing well despite the challenges.

Unfortunately, most people don't give this any thought, and as a result end up feeling unfulfilled in their relationships with mentors. I can tell you from personal experience that, if your mentors do not have the specific characteristics and personality traits that will support you in this season of your career, it will hinder you and reinforce 3D feelings of discontentment, defeat, and doubt. When this happens, it can be easy to blame yourself, and think that you're doing something wrong, when in fact it's simply a case of mismatched strengths and personality types!

At one point in my corporate career, I was struggling to find the confidence to speak up in my role. I was quiet during team meetings because I was afraid I didn't have anything intelligent to contribute. One of my sponsors was great at speaking up and attended most of the meetings I was a part of, but he never pushed me to step out of my comfort zone. If he had said, "Okay, Devika, I am challenging you to speak up and contribute your perspective during two meetings next week," I might have hated it, but I also probably would have done it, because I would have been accountable to someone other than myself.

In other seasons, I was burned out, frustrated by horrible leadership, and really struggling. In those seasons, I needed a mentor who could hear me out and offer actionable advice without judging me or adding to my dread. A mentor who pushed me and held me accountable to concrete action steps would have made things worse for me, not better.

So, as you go through this exercise, put some real thought into it. It's vastly important to engage people based on where you are and what you need so you can help them help you. You don't want to waste a mentor's time if they're not actually adding value for you, and you don't want to jeopardize a positive relationship by inviting resentment or frustration. Being mindful of this is a very mature approach.

Finally, after going through all the steps above, I want you to list three potential mentors that come to mind for you to approach based on the criteria you just identified. Once you've identified these mentors, commit to reaching out to them within the next three weeks.

Sponsors Brainstorm

Just as you did in the mentor brainstorm section above, write down your overall goal for engaging a sponsor. Remember, a sponsor is someone who actively champions you and advocates for you, so your goal should include how they can do that. Unlike with a mentor, your goal will not be "learning opportunities" or "learning a new function," but rather a clear ask on how this sponsor can get you to the opportunity you're trying to attain.

To continue the example used above, the person moving from sales to product might write, "Help me transition industries from sales into product"—which is different from "Learn about the shift from sales to product," their ask for a mentor. Your ask from a sponsor needs to be clear and concise. They should know exactly what you need, and exactly what they can do to help you get there.

Once you've set your goal, write down what you will need from this sponsor. For example, our example person might write, "Introduce me to leaders in the product organization and actively share why my skills are transferable so I'm seen as a strong candidate for open roles." If you share a statement like this with a sponsor, they will immediately know what you need and understand if they can, in fact, help you, or if there might be someone better suited to the sponsor role.

Next, write down the time commitment you're asking for. Because sponsors take a more active role in your career progression compared to mentors, it's important to have consistent time with them. I recommend meeting with your sponsor for no less than forty-five minutes bi-monthly. During your time together, you can provide updates on what you're working on, share updated versions of your executive summary, share open roles you're interested in, and get their feedback on how they can champion your work and help you move the needle toward your goal. Consistency with sponsors is key.

Now, write down the strengths you need your sponsor to have. For example, "This person is respected and has good relationships with leaders who work in product internally." Not everyone with seniority has the respect, relationships, and resources you need to meet your goals. In general, sponsors should be respected and trusted by fellow leaders to ensure their recommendations and feedback are taken seriously.

Next, consider the characteristics you need your sponsor to have. As you did in the mentor brainstorming section, consider personality traits and leadership styles. What will match your needs in this season of your career? In general, honesty, transparency, and reliability are always necessary traits to look for in a sponsor.

Finally, write down three people who come to mind as potential sponsors, and commit to approaching them within three weeks of today.

I'm often asked, "Can I have more than one sponsor?" Absolutely! Having two (or more) people in your corner, as long as they meet the criteria you just outlined, will position you better. However, remember that you will need to actively prepare for these engagements and manage the relationships so they don't fizzle. This takes time and intention, so if having more than one sponsor compromises the way you are able to show up in these relationships, I highly suggest sticking with one at a time.

Career Allies Brainstorm

Your career allies brainstorm will differ from your mentors and sponsors brainstorms in key ways.

Begin by writing down your goal for engaging career allies. For example, the person I've been using as an example might write, "Provide credibility and referral to successfully move from sales to product."

Next, write down what help you need from them specifically. Do you need to shadow their calls, receive feedback on a specific project or skill set you're building, influence decision-makers, or proactively forward positive feedback to your manager? Brainstorm all the ways in which you could work with career allies to further your goals.

Now, identify what actions you need your career allies to take to highlight you proactively or enhance your skill sets. This part is important. You must paint a picture of the exact action you need career allies to take to support you so you can communicate it to them when you approach them to be a career ally. Most of your peers will not know on their own how to be effective in a career ally role, so you will need to guide them, particularly with regard to what and how they share about you—for example, how you're taking initiative to learn another role within your company, how you're creating a productive and trusting team culture, how you're mentoring people on the team—or how they provide feedback on your strengths and skills.

(Bonus tip: leverage your career allies' feedback in LinkedIn recommendations! Positive feedback shared this way is doubly powerful because it exists on your public profile, which is your online professional brand. When recruiters or hiring managers are looking you up, they will see all of that good feedback from your career allies on your profile. So, as your career allies share positive feedback about you through email or other internal communication, you can say, "Your feedback was so thoughtfully written that I would love to have it as a part of my online professional brand through my profile. Would you mind posting it as a recommendation on LinkedIn?")

Now, let's move on to your part in the relationship. Let's write down how *you* will reinforce what you're working on. Sure, your career allies will help you—but how can you highlight the extra mile you're going to position yourself for your career goal by working with career allies? It's important to highlight your tenacity and hustle, too. This is what makes working with career allies different than working with mentors and sponsors. When working with career allies, you will need to track and reinforce their feedback. Every time your career allies send a positive email about you, file it away for later use. If they send positive feedback through your internal chat messenger, screenshot it and save it in the folder. Then, you can reinforce this feedback by reminding your manager during one-to-one meetings and performance reviews. In a performance evaluation, you can attach copies of those emails and screenshots alongside your self-evaluation. You can also remind your manager about these positive notes from career allies by sharing them as a "win for the week" when you meet. (More on "wins for the week" to come.) Remember, your visibility is your responsibility. Great leaders will make note of all the wonderful things your career allies share about you, but passive leaders will not. So, make sure you, not they, are driving the narrative about your work and potential.

Now that you've gotten clear on what actions you need your career allies to take, highlight the characteristics you need them to have. Trustworthiness, good relationships with decision-makers, and the ability to offer constructive criticism are overall important traits for career allies to have.

Lastly, write down three people you can approach to be career allies based on your brainstorm, and commit to approaching them within three weeks. Remember, trust is an important factor of having a career ally, so listen to your gut. If you do not believe this person genuinely wants to help you, please do not force it.

Initiating Relationships

The brainstorming you just did is the easiest part of building your personal network of advocates. Engaging with them and managing these relationships, however, will take intentionality, organization, preparation, and consistency. There is a specific formula that I find works well when approaching and engaging potential advocates. This not only sets the tone for the type of person you are, but also sets the expectation that you will be worth their time and investment.

We're going to engage your personal network of advocates in three stages: ask, prepare, and acknowledge.

Ask

When approaching mentors, sponsors, and career allies, ask them for their support in person or on a video call if possible. Asking through email or chat does not convey personalization. That said, you'll want to email mentors, sponsors, and career allies to give some context into why you're requesting a meeting before you make your ask. After you send context and they agree to meet, send a calendar invite to hold time for the discussion.

You can leverage the template below for your initial meeting request with mentors, sponsors, and career allies:

> *Hi, [insert name here],*
>
> *I'm reaching out because I have been thinking about career development and learning how to become more proactive about my career path. Something that resonated with me in my learning was the importance of partnering with advocates.*
>
> *You immediately came to mind because [insert your "why" for approaching this person]. I would appreciate the opportunity to share more. Are you open to scheduling a twenty-minute call to discuss how I can partner with you around my career development goals?*
>
> *Please let me know what days/times work for you, and I'll send an invite.*
>
> *Thank you,*
> *[Your signoff]*

Once you're actually in the scheduled meeting, clearly communicate why you chose this person as a possible advocate, brief them on your career goals and what you're hoping to accomplish through working with them, and share the time commitment you're asking for, including the exact amount of time you'll be meeting for and the expected duration of the partnership. For example, you might say to a mentor or career ally, "Can we agree to meet once a month for the next four months, and then reevaluate how often we will meet after that?" Sponsors generally need more time to work on your behalf, so you might say, "Is it possible to meet on the third Thursday of each month for the next eight months?"

Luckily, you just prepared for that entire conversation through the brainstorms in the previous section!

Prepare

After your mentor, sponsor, or career ally has agreed to partner with you, you'll want to prepare for every meetup or conversation. This helps your advocate know that you take this relationship seriously and value their time.

Send a calendar invitation for each meeting at least a week in advance to hold the time. (For executives, send the invite at least six weeks in advance.) Or, set permanent meeting times on the calendar (for example, on the third Monday of every month) for the duration you agreed upon in your initial commitment conversation. Being proactive about scheduling will help you avoid issues with getting on people's calendars and/or having to constantly reschedule.

About seventy-two hours before your meeting, email an agenda so the person you're meeting can be prepared for the topics you want to address. You should also send any pre-reads for context, anything you want to review together, and the exact questions you'd like your advocate to answer so they know exactly what to expect. In your first meeting, I also recommend sharing your executive summary because it provides context into who you are, what you value, and the great work you've done to date. This is especially important if you do not have a prior relationship with this person. Also, have your elevator pitch prepared and memorized in case you get the "tell me about yourself" question.

Confirm each meeting twenty-four hours in advance. There is nothing more frustrating than anticipating a meeting and preparing for it, only for the person to cancel last minute or not show up at all. Confirming the meeting will give you advance notice if the person needs to reschedule, and it will save you a lot of frustration. If you are working with an executive or someone in a high-demand role who is juggling many critical responsibilities, cancellations and reschedules are likely to happen often, so have patience and try to give them grace. However, if they consistently cancel on you without rescheduling, it's time to find another sponsor, mentor, or career ally who values your time as much as you value theirs.

Acknowledge

Always take the time to acknowledge your personal network of advocates! This part gets forgotten all the time, but it's crucial to creating a mutually satisfying relationship. Your mentors and sponsors need to know that you are present, listening, and executing on their feedback. More, they need to know that you value their time and their investment in you.

Here are some easy ways to acknowledge your advocates:

- Send a thank you email after each meeting. Mention your biggest takeaway or how you plan to act on their advice.
- Send quick updates on the results you achieve by implementing their expertise, insight, or feedback.
- Send a handwritten thank you card to communicate your appreciation, especially when you achieve what you have been working toward. You can also send a small, personalized gift if that feels aligned with your relationship.
- Write them a LinkedIn recommendation highlighting their leadership traits and how they helped you achieve your career goals.

Does this seem like a lot? It might at first, but after your first go-around, this way of showing up will feel organic. Frankly, this should be the standard of how people show up for all meetings, especially when they are the one seeking help.

To help you organize yourself as well as possible, I've created this Mentor/Sponsor Relationship checklist for you, which you can also download and print at www.devikabrij.com/thriveincolor.

The Mentor/Sponsor Relationship Checklist

Ask

- Send an email requesting an in-person meeting, video chat, or phone call to discuss the possibility of them becoming your mentor, sponsor, or career ally ☐
- Send a calendar invite including meeting location, video call link, or the phone number you will be calling them on ☐
- Prepare communication around the career goal you're working on that would benefit from their help, why you're asking them for support, why you chose them, and what time commitment will be requested ☐
- Send your potential mentor/sponsor your executive summary ☐
- Confirm your meeting twenty-four hours in advance ☐

Prepare

- Send a recurring calendar invite for the days/times you've agreed to meet (including relevant location, video call, or phone numbers) ☐
- Send agenda for upcoming meetings at least two days in advance ☐
- Prepare any updates or follow-ups from the previous meeting and share them at least two days in advance ☐
- Confirm the meeting twenty-four hours in advance ☐
- Send a thank you note within twenty-four hours of the conclusion of the meeting ☐
- Repeat the above steps for each meeting with your mentor/sponsor

Acknowledge

- Send a handwritten thank you note or card expressing your gratitude ☐
- Offer to write a testimonial or recommendation on LinkedIn or elsewhere to return the favor ☐

Approaching Mentors and Sponsors You Don't Know

I've been asked several times, "Devika, what if I don't know my prospective mentor or sponsor personally? Should I still approach them?" The answer is yes! I know it can feel intimidating to approach someone you respect and admire without a previous bond (or at least a warm introduction), but some of your greatest relationships can begin this way. I'll say it again: most people will be willing to help you if you clearly communicate why you want to engage them and what their individual skills and talents could bring to the table for you.

When approaching people you don't know personally, be sure to include the following in your initial communication:

- How this person's involvement will help you.
- What is your ask specifically? Is it a one-time phone call or consistent meetings?
- Context on yourself. (Attach your executive summary!)
- An offer of reciprocation, such as writing a testimonial on LinkedIn about how they impacted you and why you respect their work so highly.

Once you agree on a meeting time, send a calendar invite, meeting agenda, pre-read materials, and anything else that will help them get the most out of your meeting time.

This approach has worked for me personally. In fact, my current mentor is someone I had never met before I reached out. She was so impressed with my approach that she agreed to a phone call—and now, seven years later, we're still working together. You'll be surprised at who will say yes if you approach them with intention and thought.

PAY IT FORWARD

One of the most powerful and rewarding things you can do at any point in your career is to offer to be a mentor, sponsor, or career ally to other people of color. We can only win as a community if we're sending the elevator down as we make our way to each new level of our careers.

Chapter Nine

MANAGING YOUR MANAGER

SAMANTHA WAS ONE of the most senior executives I reported to at a global tech company. She was personable, but also made it known that her time was valuable. Every morning, she'd walk heavily toward her office so you could hear her from around the corner. She'd quickly wave and say, "Good morning, Devika," before sliding her glass office door closed behind her and beginning her day of back-to-back meetings.

As a project manager, I supported the more than thirty individuals on Samantha's sales team, which included numerous high-priority projects, so we met weekly on Monday mornings for thirty minutes. I didn't know at that stage in my career that I was the driver for the one-to-one meetings with my manager, so I'd make myself comfortable in her spare office chair with my laptop wide open, ready to answer Samantha's questions and create a list of things she needed from me. We typically spent the first fifteen minutes discussing updates she needed from me, and the remaining fifteen minutes discussing everything else she needed from me. If there happened to be any time left in our meetings, Samantha, through her body language and quickly moving to next steps, made it clear that she was taking the remaining time back for herself. If she felt like she had the information she needed, she would cancel without giving me the option to keep the meeting in the calendar.

Samantha never asked me if there was anything *I* wanted to discuss, or if there was anything she could do to support me. She was a high-powered executive, and her time was precious. I didn't understand that my time was precious, too, and that I had a right to ask for what I needed. My approach of "tell Samantha what I'm working on and learn what else she needs" certainly wasn't serving my career advancement, and as a result, I only spent a year in that role before moving on to another company where I felt like I had a shot for advancement. What I didn't understand was that my lack of advancement at the first company was in part the result of my own failure to create a case for my advancement. Opportunities may indeed have been there, but I hadn't set myself up to access them.

As we learned earlier in this book, 60 percent or more of your career success hinges on your ability to self-advocate and drive exposure of your values and accomplishments. So, how can you get comfortable with elevating your success consistently? The answer is to start baking exposure into your natural environment and engagements at work, especially with leaders and decision-makers, and in particular with your direct manager. In this chapter, I'll share strategies for how to do this effectively.

However, before we begin, we need to address the elephant in the room.

Advocating for yourself, sharing your wins, and showcasing your skill sets can have negative consequences for people of color, especially Black professionals. This is especially true when self-advocacy is not celebrated, expected, or ingrained in the culture and value system of your company, or if your direct manager is uncomfortable with you advocating for your work. Certain leaders may bring inherent biases and expectations around what is considered acceptable behavior from individuals of your race, gender, and level of seniority. Is this fair? Absolutely not. I wish we had the power to change people to make work environments fair and equitable for all, but the reality is we can't control the types of people we encounter in an organization. Even in companies that promote and empower a collaborative, supportive culture, not all employees will exemplify that.

So, what do *you* do?

You show up anyway. You advocate for yourself anyway. Because if you don't highlight your success, who will do it for you?

Waiting around for someone to see you, acknowledge you, and reward you is the furthest thing from strategic. So, it's time to approach self-advocacy in a way that can be digested by both the leaders who support you and the leaders who have some serious work to do in their leadership skills. You can do this by leveraging the environments where you have consistent face time with leadership—in particular, during your one-to-one meetings with your direct manager—and make these opportunities work in your favor.

MAKE YOUR MEETINGS NEEDLE-MOVERS

One-to-one meetings with your managers can be immensely beneficial if they are managed correctly by both you and your leader. They can also come with their fair share of challenges. Recognizing and understanding these challenges first is crucial for navigating these interactions effectively.

Before I show you my strategies for getting the most out of your time with managers, let's look at some of the most common factors that get in the way of effective one-to-one meetings. These include:

- Inconsistent meeting times
- Lack of preparation and/or an agenda
- Unsafe space
- Managerial skill variation
- One-sided dialogue

Inconsistent Meetings

The frequency of your one-to-one meetings might not always be consistent. In fact, in some cases, the *only* consistent things about these meetings are your manager's requests to cancel or reschedule them! I've experienced this countless times with leaders. However, this is a huge disadvantage for both you and your leader.

You need this visibility and time to dialogue with your leaders. One-to-one meetings enable you to highlight your contributions, discuss topics that are top-of-mind for both you and your leader, and seek constructive feedback so you can successfully work toward your development goals—and *you are worth that time and care.*

Additionally, since your leader is accountable for your contributions toward team and company goals, meeting with you and understanding what you're spending your time on makes their job easier—but unfortunately, some leaders do not see these engagements as a long-term benefit to them.

If you are not meeting your manager weekly, bi-weekly, or at the very least monthly, you need to ensure you receive that face time. If you're not, here is a template email to help you get those one-to-one meetings back on the calendar:

Hi, [Insert manager's name],

As you know, I've been proactively thinking about my career development here at [company name]. I realize that having consistent communication with you and giving you visibility into my work is a critical part of my development opportunities.

I noticed that you have canceled the last few one-to-one meetings we had in the calendar. I know there is a lot going on across our team, but I'd like to ask that we keep our meetings because I value my one-to-one time with you. Is there a day/time that works better for you? I'm happy to shift our meeting times to something more convenient. Please let me know your thoughts, and thanks for your time.

Sincerely,
[Your signoff]

If your workplace does not actively require managers to meet with their direct reports, do not allow this gap in judgment stop you from making the ask for your own benefit. Here is a template you can use to request a regular one-to-one meeting with your manager:

> *Hi, [Insert manager's name],*
>
> *As you know, I've been proactively thinking about my career development here at [company name]. I realize that having consistent communication with you and giving you visibility into my work is a critical part of my development opportunities. I'd like to create a space where I can highlight my work and receive your feedback on a consistent basis. Are you open to us scheduling a thirty-minute weekly or bi-weekly one-to-one meeting? I'm open to meeting on the day/time that works best for your schedule, and am happy to prepare an agenda for each meeting.*
>
> *Are you open to getting this on the calendar?*
>
> *[Your signoff]*

Most (good) leaders will be happy to give you this time. If, for some reason, your manager declines, I strongly encourage you to consider whether you should build your future in a company where leaders will not make time to understand your contributions and support your growth. You are worthy of your leader's time—and if your leader doesn't agree, there are plenty of managers elsewhere who will gladly spend time with you, understanding that one-to-one meetings are of mutual benefit between all direct reports and their managers.

Lack of Preparation and/or an Agenda

If your one-to-ones tend to be more casual, it's also possible that they lack structure, including a consistent agenda. This can lead to unproductive discussions, missed opportunities to elevate your wins and contributions, and missed opportunities to receive the help, feedback, or answers you need from your managers. Without proper preparation and structure, the meeting might become a catch-up session—or worse, a formality—rather than a meaningful exchange.

Now, there's nothing wrong with a more casual one-to-one meeting. I've known many managers who liked to grab coffee and have "walking meetings" or conversations in the office common space rather than sitting across a desk from their team members. This can be a great way to build rapport. However, since these environments are not conducive to sharing visuals, documents, or an agenda, it can feel more difficult to advocate for yourself and share your wins and asks. It also makes it more difficult to refer back to the conversation if topics need to be revisited.

If you feel like you're getting what you need from a less formal approach, I encourage you to keep the existing dynamic. However, if you're running into issues where you and your manager disagree on what was actually said, action items are not being followed through on, or you don't have the space to highlight everything you need to, it may be necessary to request a shift to a more structured setting, like a boardroom or video call. Regardless of your meeting dynamics, I encourage you to create a paper trail through pre-meeting agendas, follow-up emails, and a shared tracking document. (More on that later in this chapter.)

Unsafe Space

You may feel hesitant to express your authentic thoughts, concerns, or aspirations in one-to-one meetings due to a perceived power imbalance or personality clash between you and your leader. This can limit the openness and honesty necessary for fruitful discussions around your career aspirations and needs. As a result, the one-to-one will serve your leader's needs more than yours.

By implementing the instructions I'll present later in this chapter, as well as sharing your executive summary and career goals with your manager, you can go a long way toward correcting a power imbalance. However, if the one-to-one space is unsafe for other reasons—such as a leader's racism, sexism, or simply a challenging personality, here is how to approach it.

Keep Clear and Detailed Records

Keep detailed record of any instances, times, locations, and other people involved in each incident, along with a description of what occurred or what was said. This documentation will be necessary if you decide to escalate the situation. If you decide to confront your manager directly, such examples can also help you communicate to them why such behavior is unacceptable.

Decide How to Proceed

Make a decision as to how you want to approach the situation. Do you want to give your leader the benefit of the doubt and proceed as if they don't know their behavior is problematic? Or do you want to go straight into formal proceedings?

The only way to make this decision is to trust your discernment. Do you feel safe to have a challenging and vulnerable conversation with this person? Is this person deliberately attempting to harm, minimize, control, or belittle you, or are they truly unaware of the impact of their actions on you and others?

We all know well-meaning individuals who are ignorant as to how their behaviors impact marginalized people. This isn't about making excuses for them, but rather about deciding whether you feel comfortable pointing out their problematic words and actions through clear, open communication. If you decide to go this route, you're giving them a chance to correct their behavior before getting HR involved. Your record of examples will support you if you decide to have such a conversation.

Here are two examples of how I handled problematic colleagues.

As I've shared in previous chapters, at one point in my early career I worked on a team completely comprised of women of color. As a client account manager, we worked closely with a designated partner to sell marketing products to clients and manage client relationships. My colleague Kennedy was paired with Geoff, an older white man who often made inappropriate comments. However, it was evident that he didn't have ulterior motives and didn't mean to be problematic; he was just straight-up ignorant.

One day, Geoff approached me in the office and asked me, "Do you know what those weird Christians call the end of the world?"

It was a totally random question and I was thrown off. I wondered, *Why is he asking me this, out of everyone here?* I have never hidden my Christian faith, and found it offensive that he was calling Christians "weird."

I responded, "No idea, Geoff," and turned back to my computer screen, but he wasn't deterred.

"The rapture! That's it. Just came back to me. Thanks!"

What the hell just happened? I thought. But it was so comical that my irritation evaporated.

The next week, at a team dinner, Geoff crossed another boundary. He asked me, "Devi, where do you live?" When I mentioned my neighborhood, an upscale and desirable part of Toronto, he was shocked. "That's an expensive area!"

The tone wasn't, "Way to go, Devika!" It was more, "How do *you* live *there*?"

"Yup. I like it," I replied, before changing the topic. To be honest, I was so used to my "naive" white peers making comments like this that it barely phased me anymore.

Several days later, while in a meeting with a group of key clients, Geoff turned to Kennedy and asked, "Can you go make a pot of coffee?"

This was wildly offensive. Kennedy wasn't an assistant. She was a strategic partner to Geoff. His request was blatantly sexist and belittling to Kennedy both as a woman and as a person of color. What was stopping Geoff from making his own damn coffee?

Not wanting to be confrontational, Kennedy forced a smile and left to make the coffee. She found me on her way to the kitchen, and I could tell she was seething.

"What happened?" I asked.

She explained, with every possible curse word flying out of her mouth. She was pissed off, and rightfully so. With one ignorant question, Geoff had just reduced her authority and position with their clients, undermined her value to the team, and made her feel like he didn't see her as a partner.

The next day, Geoff and I were the first in the office. I asked him if we could chat before the rest of the team arrived. I wanted him to know that the conversation would be private so he wouldn't be embarrassed. We sat down, and I began by asking, "Are you open to some feedback?"

He was thrown off, but agreed to listen.

"I wanted to have a private conversation because of a few incidents in the past couple of weeks that have made me and others on the team uncomfortable. I know you're a good person and wouldn't intentionally hurt anyone, so I wanted to bring this directly to you. The other day, you asked me a question, referring to Christians as weird. As the only person on this team who's outward with her faith, this made me uncomfortable. I brushed it off, but …"

Geoff profusely apologized. "I didn't mean it that way."

"Thanks, but can I finish before our peers arrive?"

He nodded.

"I brushed it off because I knew you didn't mean to be offensive. But the other day, you asked Kennedy to make a pot of coffee in front of clients. She was really upset. I'm sure you were just trying to attend to the clients' needs, but asking your female peer to make coffee instead of handling it yourself portrayed her as an assistant, not your strategic partner and equal. I'm assuming you didn't mean to do that, and that you didn't realize the harm it caused, but I wanted to point it out so you're more aware. I'd hate for your reputation or brand among the team to be impacted without you realizing it."

Geoff looked both embarrassed and relieved. He thanked me for sharing, and apologized.

Geoff's behavior didn't change overnight, but it did change. Over time, he became more sensitive and aware, and even asked for support in situations he wasn't sure how to navigate. If Geoff had had a pompous, narcissistic, or controlling demeanor, I would have considered escalating the situation to HR and filing a formal report. But I felt safe with him. I wanted to give him the chance to do better before I took that step.

Then, there was Rick, my partner on client accounts.

In my opinion, Rick was an awful person. He treated me like I was his assistant. He didn't take my recommendations, undermined me in front of clients, and was generally pompous and nasty. He once called me "sweetie" in front of a client while openly laughing at my suggestions.

For a while, I bottled up my anger and frustration, only venting to my direct team and staying focused on my job. However, Rick's behavior soon started to affect the whole team.

Nev joined our team remotely from New York in an entry-level role, and was much younger than most of us. When she came to visit for an in-person meeting, Rick rolled in thirty minutes late and with a big attitude. I don't recall exactly what happened, but when Nev made a small error that could have been easily corrected, Rick went ballistic on her, raising his voice and getting in her face to the point where Nev looked legitimately scared.

"There's no need to yell," I interjected. "We're all professionals, and there isn't going to be any yelling on this team."

To be honest, I was surprised by my assertiveness. But by that point I'd had it with Rick's bullshit.

Rick slammed his notebook on the glass table, got up, and walked out of the room. His behavior had always been questionable, but this was totally unacceptable, and I worried that it would only get worse. So, I went to HR. We were forced into mediation with both of our managers and the HR manager assigned to our team. I was prepared with documentation of several examples of Rick's horrible behavior.

Rick had nothing to say beyond, "Devika, you're such a bitch."

As they say, the proof is in the pudding. After the HR manager picked her jaw up off the floor, she condemned his language and put him on a strict performance plan. A few months later, he was terminated.

I won't lie, the whole process was intimidating. I still had to work with Rick while the company got their ducks in order to terminate him. Every time I had to be in a room with him, I felt shaky. I was also resentful that it took my manager, Rick's manager, and HR so long to terminate him when his behavior had impacted so many employees.

In summary, discerning and gut-checking before deciding how to proceed with a complaint will always help you find the best path. Geoff was willing and able to change, but if I'd tried to have a private conversation with Rick before reporting him, I believe it would have made the situation even more untenable.

Review Your Company's Policies on Harassment and Discrimination

If you decide to escalate, be prepared. Review your company's policies on discrimination and harassment, and be sure you understand the correct procedures for reporting these incidents. You don't want to be dismissed or for your case to be put on a back burner because you're underprepared.

Involve Someone You Trust

Share your concerns with a trusted leader or in-company mentor/sponsor who can provide you with support and advice. They can offer perspective on the best course of action, and may even be able to intervene on your behalf.

Consider External Resources

If the problem persists after you've talked to your manager directly or if HR is showing signs that they are going to protect the manager and make you the problem, consider contacting external resources like an employment lawyer who can help you understand next steps. Most lawyers will offer a free or minimal-fee consultation. This can be a worthwhile investment if you're feeling unsafe.

Managerial Skill Variation

Not all managers are equally skilled in conducting effective one-to-one meetings. Some might lack the ability to provide constructive feedback, engage in meaningful and mutually beneficial discussions, or set clear goals, which can hinder the overall effectiveness of the meeting. In these situations, you especially need to be the driver of your one-to-one conversations to fill the communication gap. The tools you'll learn in this chapter will be of great help to you in such a scenario.

One-Sided Dialogue

For many underrepresented professionals, a one-to-one meeting can feel like a run-through of the list of what they are working on for their manager's visibility, and that's it. As a result, you may feel that your meetings are for your leader's knowledge and benefit, and that you're simply there to deliver the information they need. This is the furthest thing from the truth. The one-to-one meeting should be a mutually beneficial time for you and your manager to discuss topics that are top-of-mind for both of you. Your manager should walk away with the information they need about your deliverables, but you should also have the opportunity to highlight your wins and contributions, and to seek help and feedback.

***

Whether you resonate with any of these challenges or are dealing with one that's not listed, I'm here to tell you that your one-to-one meetings are too important to feel unproductive, unsuccessful, or like a waste of time. When navigated the right way, these engagements can have career-altering effects.

Let's explore what that can look like.

CREATING AN EFFECTIVE AND BENEFICIAL ONE-TO-ONE MEETING

An effective and successful one-to-one meeting is one where both you and your manager gain what you need from the conversation. For you, that looks like having space to share your contributions and accomplishments, brief your manager on how you're driving toward team and company goals through the scope of your role, and seeking feedback or help when needed, including around your career development.

For your manager, this looks like understanding the progress of the initiatives you're working on, the challenges and successes you're experiencing, any threats to meeting the objectives that need to be resolved, and any results and impact they can communicate up the chain so that high-level leaders know how all teams are driving toward the overall company priority.

Clearly, there are intersections between what you need and what your manager needs, but there are differences, too. So, how do you create an environment and agenda that delivers the needs of both individuals and can be completed in thirty minutes if needed?

Here's how you do it:

- Create consistency
- Track information
- Design an effective agenda

As we discussed earlier, you should be meeting with your leader weekly or bi-weekly for at least thirty minutes, or once a month at the minimum. The agenda categories, pre-meeting discussion, and follow-up should also be consistent. This creates alignment between you and your leader on what will be discussed, what information should be prepared in advance, and what both parties should be coming to the table ready to talk about.

Next, all information shared in your one-to-one meetings should be tracked in a shared document like a Google Sheet. This document will be accessible to both you and your leader and contain the topics that were discussed in every one-to-one. Not only will this catalogue the work you're doing week after week, your weekly wins, and the asks you've made of your leader, it will also come in handy when it's time for performance reviews and self-assessments where you need to recall all of your contributions for the quarter, the half, or the year.

Finally, a meeting without a consistent agenda and expectations of what will be discussed carries no momentum beyond the meeting itself. Therefore, there needs to be regularity in the meeting agenda and the categories that will be discussed. This creates an expectation that certain topics will be covered, and makes space for important pieces of your self-advocacy that might otherwise be crowded out by other objectives.

As someone who has experienced great and not so great one-to-one's that ultimately impacted my access to opportunities, I've paid attention to what makes one-to-ones impactful. During my time in corporate, I created my own meeting agendas that I leveraged with my leaders. When I was managing a team, I asked my direct reports to use the same template because it was incredibly efficient. This template is now something I introduce to my clients in my consulting work, and it's proven to be a game-changer for many professionals and their leaders.

THE BRIJ THE GAP ONE-TO-ONE MEETING AGENDA

These are the four categories you need to include in every one-to-one meeting (aka, your agenda) that will foster mutually beneficial and collaborative conversations while enabling you to increase your exposure:

- Wins
- Inform
- Discuss
- Ask

Wins

Start each one-to-one meeting by sharing a win you've had since your last one-to-one. This might include completing your part of a project, event, or objective successfully; a positive client or peer testimonial; a milestone you've achieved; or an action you took on feedback that ended up with a positive result. Essentially, it's something you're proud of and want to highlight to your manager. Not only does this drive exposure to the good work you're doing, but it also creates an expectation with your manager that you will proactively take ownership over your good work.

When self-advocacy feels like a challenge, setting the expectation that you will be sharing a key win in each one-to-one meeting will actually make it easier for you because you will simply be speaking to a topic on your shared meeting agenda. You can also use the template below to inform your manager of your intentions and ask for support:

> *Hi, [insert manager's name],*
>
> *I'm currently exploring how I can overcome my challenge of feeling self-conscious about sharing my contributions to the team. I wanted to share with you that self-advocacy is a challenge for me. So, to help me grow in this area, I'll be sharing a win with you in every one-to-one meeting that showcases something I'm proud about or something I want to highlight that is going very well. How do you feel about that?*
>
> *Thanks, and I look forward to your feedback.*
>
> *[Your signoff]*

I doubt any leader will say no to that. In fact, most managers will likely love to hear that! Sharing your wins at the start of every one-to-one conversation and setting expectations of that time together will strengthen your self-advocacy muscle over time. It will also show your leader that you are confident and know your worth, which will translate into success in having your needs met.

One tip here: pay attention to the facial expressions, body language, and overall response of your leader when you're sharing your wins. Are they as energetic about those wins as you are, or do they seem unenthused by what you're sharing? If your manager is the type that naturally lacks expression or is good at concealing emotion, this may be hard to gauge, but in most cases, you should be able to tell if they resonate with what you're sharing. If it appears they are not, that's an indication that your idea of a win doesn't match theirs. This isn't a problem, but it is something you should be aware of. After all, we are all different humans, and how we measure success also differs. My suggestion in such a case is that you should still feel empowered to share what matters to you, even if your leader doesn't view it as a win equally, but also pay attention to what your leader *does* qualify as a win so you can integrate those examples, too. If you're not sure how your manager is feeling, seek understanding by saying something like, "What types of wins that I've shared have resonated with you the most?" Based on their response, you will have a deeper understanding of what they deem a win.

Inform

After you share your win(s), it's time to inform your manager of all the high-level updates you owe them. This is a bird's eye view of the aspects of the work and projects you're managing that they will care about. In most one-to-ones, your manager doesn't need context on every single item on your plate. Some responsibilities are higher priority and therefore require more dialogue, but unnecessary discussion takes time and energy away from other topics like your career development or the help you need from your manager.

One helpful strategy is to list out all the items you're currently working on in your meeting agenda and the latest status update so your manager can glance over them and zero in on what is most important to them. This gives your projects the visibility they need without taking up more time than necessary in a one-to-one.

Discuss

In the "discuss" portion of your one-to-one, you will dive into items you're managing that require more dialogue or visibility. These are probably also what your manager cares about the most.

Typically, a one-to-one meeting is thirty minutes, so you won't have time to deep dive into every single thing on your plate, nor do you really need to spend your time that way. That's why the "Inform" section above helps you track and communicate all that you're managing while the "discuss" section helps you use your time strategically to discuss the more high-priority items.

Asks

Make sure to save time at the end of the meeting to make asks of your manager. This is your opportunity to get what you need from your manager, versus keeping the conversation about what they need from you.

Your asks could include items like help with a project you're working on, feedback that you need, or following up on a previous career conversation. Carving this time out of the one-to-one creates the expectation that, just as much as you are accountable to your manager, they are accountable to you as your leader. Like your wins, the practice of "asks" will get easier with time as you practice your self-advocacy skills.

Creating Alignment in Your One-to-One Agenda

When communicating your wins, inform, and discuss sections, you will want to align your agenda items to current company or team goals, but also to the areas you are measured on during performance reviews, the expected responsibilities of your current role, or the responsibilities of the next role or level of seniority you're seeking. Ask yourself, "What do I need to provide to my manager weekly, monthly, and quarterly to prove I'm ready for what I'm asking for?"

Here are some simple examples:

- If your goal is building your professional brand, you'll need to prove areas of skills and strengths around what you want to be known for.
- If your goal is to move into a management position, you'll want to prove that you're an effective leader on the team and a driver of corporate culture and values.
- If your goal is promotion, you'll want to provide examples of what you are doing or have done to show that you have the necessary skills to be successful in the specific role you're seeking.

This is where the real strategy comes into play with regard to your one-to-one meetings. If you're operating in a task-based approach, using your one-to-one time to list off all the tasks you're doing and discussing only those items, how far are you really moving the needle in your career? You only get a short amount of solo time with your managers, so you need to use that time the *right* way—meaning, in a way that aligns with your goals for your current and future career, not just with the goals of your manager, team, or company.

Tracking and Reinforcing Feedback

Whenever you receive feedback or next steps for anything relating to career development during one-to-one meetings, recap it in an email after the meeting, bcc yourself, and file it away in a folder.

Why do you need to do this? Because you want to ensure that both you and your leader are aligned on feedback, answers to your questions, and next steps to avoid any misunderstanding, misremembering, or outright blindsiding that may occur in the aftermath of your one-to-one conversations. You need to show that you are holding your leader to their word, and also create a paper trail to which you can refer later if there is any discrepancy. A situation where it's your word against that of your manager will rarely go well for you.

Unfortunately, being blindsided and/or gaslit with regard to what transpires in one-to-one conversations is a common experience for underrepresented people in the workplace. They believe they are aligned with their manager on feedback and next steps but later realize this isn't the reality. Typically, this unfolds in a way that isn't fair to them.

I'm sure you have been there. I know I have.

Remember my manager, Heather, about whom I shared in Chapters Two and Eight? In addition to our other clashes, she and other leadership took advantage of my lack of a paper trail to force me out of my role.

Early after I accepted a role in another department working at that large social media company in Toronto, my new manager, Kelly, asked me if I'd be open to moving to New York City, where most of the team was located (including Shannon, a manipulative senior colleague who I introduced you to in Chapter Eight and the initiator of my eventual termination. More to come on that later!). I asked if this move was a requirement, and she said no, but it was preferred. I told her I would consider it and get back to her within a few weeks.

Now, I'd moved to Toronto in part to be close to family, and I took care of my grandmother on the weekends. Moving would not allow me to continue that commitment. I did give the idea some consideration because it excited me, but ultimately decided against it. Instead, I would stay in Toronto and committed to flying to New York once a month to meet in person with the team.

Kelly said she understood and was aligned to the plan of how I'd grow connection to my team through frequent travel, and that was the end of that—or so I thought.

Shortly after that, Kelly left for an extended leave of absence, and I got a new manager—Heather. Within a few months, Heather was already compiling a running list of what I was doing "wrong," including my travel arrangements in New York for in-person team meetings, which I shared in Chapter Two. (This was largely based on feedback from Shannon. More on that later.)

Eight months later, Kelly came back. One of her first priorities was to schedule catch-up one-to-one meetings with the entire team. Everyone seemed to have pleasant conversations with her—but not me. I hadn't talked to Kelly in months, but the very first question she aggressively posed was, "Why haven't you moved to New York City? You know that was a requirement of you getting this job."

I was stunned. I recapped our previous conversation that the move to New York was preferred but not mandatory, and that I had received her blessing on my decision to stay in Toronto. But Kelly, who had debriefed with Heather, was now looking for an excuse to push me out, largely based on Heather's negative feedback. She replied, "Devika, no. That's not what we agreed on."

I was beyond shocked. How could the script flip so quickly? The conversation ended with her telling me that if I didn't agree to move to New York, I'd have to leave the role—end of story. I was furious. They couldn't eliminate me from the team for bad performance or anything else of actual substance, but it was Kelly's (and Heather's) word against mine at this point, and it didn't look good for me.

I often wonder if things would have been different if I'd gotten ahead of this by recapping the conversation regarding my move when it happened. My follow-up email could have read something like this:

Hey, Kelly,

Thank you for taking the time to discuss a possible move to New York City with me today. I appreciate you confirming that this was a preference but not a requirement, and that you understand the family values and reasoning behind my decision to stay in Toronto and care for my grandmother. As we discussed, I will travel to New York once per month to spend time with the team in person.

If I had somehow misunderstood the conversation between us (which I absolutely did not), Kelly would have had the opportunity to write back and clarify her position on the matter. Later, when she was challenging me—and quite frankly calling me a liar—I could have used that recap email to prove that the conversation occurred in the way I explained. But, because I was newer to my career and didn't know that such paper trails could be necessary, I had nothing to prove my position—and, sure enough, I was forced out of my role just a few months later.

That's just one example of why recap emails are vitally important after any one-to-one conversation, and in particular any conversation that can impact your career. The story I just shared was an extreme example, but recap emails can also support you in more common work situations. For instance, let's say that you initiate a conversation about a promotion during your weekly one-to-ones, and your manager says, "I need to see A, B, and C from you in order to give you this promotion." You agree, and commit to working on the areas highlighted. Then the much-anticipated time arrives, but you don't get the promotion because, all of a sudden, the goalposts have moved. You're now hearing your manager say he needs to see you do X, Y, and Z to be promoted—and the original items from your previous conversations are no longer even on the list! This is extremely frustrating and a recipe for generating 3D feelings.

So, what if you had recapped your manager's feedback from the very beginning? Although it wouldn't prevent him from changing his mind, it would keep him accountable to the feedback he's given and the goalposts he'd set with regard to your promotion.

In such a case, your recap email might look like this:

Hi, [insert manager's name],

Thank you so much for taking the time to talk with me about my promotion today during our one-to-one. You communicated that you need me to highlight more examples of how I successfully operate in A, B, and C for me to be promoted. As a next step, I will be sharing more context in upcoming meetings about how I'm working toward this area to keep me on track for the promotion.

If I've gotten any part of your feedback incorrect, please let me know. Thank you for your commitment to my success!

[Your signoff]

This not only creates a paper trail for you, but it also binds your leader to what he said. When it's time for a promotion conversation, it will be a lot harder for him to move the goalposts on you because you've been tracking and reinforcing your work through the items on your one-to-one agenda that you've been sharing weekly. It also gives you a framework for asking for the promotion you have earned if your current manager leaves his position, either temporarily or permanently.

You don't need to send a recap email for every conversation you have with your leader, but I encourage you to make this a practice for *any* feedback or discussion that impacts your career path, access to opportunities, or other major decisions. Unfortunately, blindsiding, gaslighting, or constantly moving goalposts are more of a challenge for underrepresented professionals than for others, but this simple practice can go a long way toward minimizing negative effects on your career.

The One-to-One Shared Document

Earlier, I mentioned creating a shared document to track your one-to-one conversations with your manager. In this section, you'll find a template to use to create that document.

I prefer to use Google Sheets for shared documents, because they are always up to date and can be shared with the click of a link, but you can also use an Excel spreadsheet if you prefer.

This document is broken up into clear columns under which you will be tracking information related to your one-to-one meetings. For ease, you can download a Google Sheets template at www.devikabrij.com/thriveincolor. Or, create your own by setting up the columns like this:

A	B	C	D	E
Date	**Category**	**Update/ Notes**	**Due Date**	**Questions/Feedback from Manager**

Let's walk through each column.

- *Column A: Date.* The date your one-to-one is occurring.

- *Column B: Category.* The category of what you're reporting in column C—meaning, wins, inform topics, discussion topics, or asks. So, if you're sharing a win in column C, you'll want to label that update as "win" in column B. If you're including updates on high-visibility projects in column C that you need to spend time discussing, you'll want to label that update as "discuss" in column B. This allows you to sort and filter the spreadsheet for easier reporting during evaluations or career conversations. This is a handy way to track all the good work you're doing while simultaneously briefing your leaders on them in real time during your one-to-one's. Since this is a shared doc, your manager will have access to this as well and can do the same thing, so it's a win-win.

- *Column D: Due Date.* This column is optional. It is for due dates you assign to your manager for items you need help with, or due dates your manager assigns for items or progress they need from you. For example, if you ask your manager to help you with something specific on a project, you can assign a due date so they know the deadline you're working with. This is helpful, but not mandatory.
- *Column E: Questions/Feedback from Manager.* This column is also optional. This is where your manager can input any questions or comments before you meet for your one-to-one, or offer feedback after your one-to-one. If they review this shared document before your one-to-one, they can plan ahead by inputting their questions and comments into the doc itself to make your meeting more productive. In my experience, some managers use this section, and others won't; it depends on how proactive or organized they are.

So, there you have it: the official Brij the Gap One-to-One Meeting Agenda. In my experience, it's been a game-changer for most people who have used it. I know it will be every bit as powerful for you.

A Few Helpful Hints

- *Choose a shared document that works for your internal systems.* If your company uses Google, use Google Sheets. If they use Microsoft, use Excel. If you do not have document sharing capacities, simply use the platform of your choice and share the updated document with your manager weekly.
- *Leverage this document whether your manager uses it or not.* The key here is to track your accomplishments weekly so you can reinforce and reiterate your value during your one-to-ones. Google Sheets and Excel will help you sort data more efficiently than other formats. For example, if it's time for your annual performance evaluation, you can go into your one-to-one doc and filter out all of your wins, discuss sections, and inform sections so you have a complete view of all your accomplishments in one view. Using the information, you can write a thorough self-assessment, ensuring you have not missed including something that should be highlighted. (Google Docs, OneNote, and Microsoft Word do not give you this option.)

- *Don't delete past meeting items and agendas!* You are adding to your document each week over time to create a running record of your accomplishments. You can, however, start a new "sheet" within the document for each new year if you want to keep things streamlined.
- *Create a backup.* If you are using a shared document with your manager, create a private backup copy that you update regularly. If someone accidentally deletes or overwrites key information, you don't want to lose your records and hard work! Version histories can only go so far, so a separately named file is best for backup. Alternately, you can download and email the document to yourself each week once you update it.
- *Celebrate what you've achieved.* Another goal of this document is to remind you of all of your accomplishments and achievements so you can confidently express your value in key conversations, performance reviews, self-assessments, and interviews. When you're moving too fast or doing too much in your role, it can be easy to let things slip by. More, most people can't remember all that they've worked on over the course of longer periods of time, so this format gives you everything you need to know at a glance.

***

I hope that, after reading this chapter, you've realized that your one-to-one isn't just another meeting on your calendar to review tasks with your manager. It can be incredibly powerful if you leverage it strategically. By taking into consideration the information I've shared here and incorporating the one-to-one template into your meetings with your leaders, you'll be in a much more powerful position to advocate for your needs by highlighting your successes and tracking your contributions in a way that cannot be argued with.

I encourage you to create and implement the one-to-one agenda as soon as possible so you can be in a powerful position to drive your career forward.

Chapter Ten

CONQUERING YOUR PERFORMANCE EVALUATION

SHAY ALWAYS DREADED her bi-annual company-wide performance reviews. Although she performed well consistently throughout the year, she felt overwhelmed trying to summarize all of her accomplishments and career goals into two forty-five-minute conversations a year.

Shay, like most, didn't leverage her one-to-one time with her manager, Ben, as well as she could. She typically talked about her running list of tasks and status updates during weekly meetings, leaving no time to discuss feedback or topics that were top-of-mind for her. Ben always complimented her on how she managed her heavy workload, so in Shay's mind she was in great standing, which made her feel confident. However, that confidence—as well as her trust in Ben—went out the window during a recent end-of-year performance evaluation.

Shay spent over a week putting together examples of what she had accomplished over the previous six months, and filled out the required self-assessment sheet, on which she was asked to list her achievements and what she wanted to highlight about her performance. Then, she had to rate herself as "not meeting expectations," "meeting expectations," or "exceeding expectations" in multiple categories of strengths, competencies, and corporate culture and values. Not wanting to appear arrogant, Shay selected "meeting expectations" for most items and "exceeding expectations" for strengths she knew enabled her to do her job well. After all, she was managing nearly 20 percent more work volume than her peers due to unexpected turnover on her team—and, despite this, was still able to meet every key performance indicator.

During the performance review conversation with her manager, Shay presented her self-assessment and rating, confident that her manager would agree. After all, he had never communicated anything but praise to Shay, not even constructive criticisms. However, as soon as Ben entered the meeting room, Shay knew the energy was off. Ben didn't seem to react positively to the examples she shared regarding her accomplishments. He just sat there, stoic and unimpressed. Finally, he said, "Thank you for sharing, Shay. You have certainly stepped up this year for the team and helped us manage the workload even though we still need to hire two team members. I really appreciate your dedication. But I'm afraid we do not align on the quality of the work you are producing."

Shay's throat dropped to her stomach. "My 'quality of work'?" she asked. "Can you explain?"

Ben went on to say that she lacked attention to detail, and that sometimes the data would be slightly off on the reports she delivered. Not always, just sometimes. What Shay marked as "exceeding expectations," Ben had marked as "not meeting expectations."

What Shay wanted to say in that moment was, "You've never once in the last year mentioned my data was incorrect! You thanked me for stepping up and delivering despite the fact that the company hadn't gotten it together and hired much-needed help. Why is this coming up now, during my performance review?" But, as a Black woman, she felt that she had to be especially careful of how she reacted to ensure nobody associated her with the "Angry Black Woman" stereotype. So, instead, she said, "I see. I'll try to be more thorough." Frustrated and on the verge of tears, she still managed to smile through it.

You see, Shay knew the reality of what was going on. Even if she made some mistakes, she was still a solid performer and a team player. She never complained about the workload because she wanted to prove she could handle more responsibilities and make a case for her salary increase conversation. This performance evaluation of "not meeting expectations" would make it harder for her to get the promotion she deserved. If Ben had flagged incorrect reports throughout the year, she would have been able to slow down, be more diligent, and perhaps ask for help to offload some of the work she'd taken on. Now, though, she would have to prove herself in new ways, delaying her promotion and rebuilding the narrative around her work contributions. All of this could have been avoided if Ben had simply communicated—but, he hadn't. As a result, Shay was deflated, her trust in Ben was gone, and she ended up being the next person on the team to leave the company.

For better or worse, performance evaluations are not passive career conversations. They dictate your future within a company and the opportunities you will have access to. Every company has their own version of how performance is tracked, how feedback is given, how often reviews occur, and even what they are called. (Some names include self-assessments, performance reviews, goal-setting conversations, 360 reviews, performance evaluations, and so many more.) For the sake of simplicity, we will call these reviews "performance evaluations" in this chapter.

Performance evaluations typically occur twice a year—at the half, and again at the end or very beginning of the year. I've also known some companies to hold a formal check-in every quarter to ensure goals are being set and measured in shorter increments of time throughout the year. No matter how often your company mandates a performance evaluation, it's important that *you* are driving these career conversations to set yourself up for successful career development and advancement. While most people believe that preparation for performance evaluations should happen just before your manager schedules the conversation, this is a huge mistake. Preparation should occur throughout the year, and you should plan to have several career check-in conversations leading up to the formal, company-wide reviews.

Also, there are great benefits to performance evaluations that many professionals overlook. Just a few of these benefits are:

- *Feedback and clarity.* Evaluations provide you with feedback on your job performance so you know where you stand. This feedback can help you understand your strengths and areas that need improvement, leading to personal and professional growth.
- *Alignment with goals.* Performance evaluations ensure that employees' work aligns with the organization's goals and objectives. By reviewing performance

against predetermined criteria, organizations can ensure that their workforce is working toward shared goals. Performance evaluations offer the opportunity to highlight and refine how you're driving toward those goals within the scope of your role.

- *Recognition and motivation.* Positive feedback and recognition for a job well done can boost your morale and motivation. This can lead to increased job satisfaction and productivity.
- *Identification of development needs.* Performance evaluations help identify areas where you may need additional training or development. If you work for a company that values this, they will likely provide you with resources, education, and opportunities to ensure you excel in your role.
- *Rewards and incentives:* Performance evaluations often inform decisions about promotions, raises, and bonuses. The data you and your leader provide is valuable for senior leadership who are approving and signing off on these important decisions.
- *Legal documentation:* In some cases, performance evaluations can serve as legal documentation of an employee's performance. This can be important in situations involving termination without cause. If you have a history of strong performance evaluations and are suddenly terminated, you may be able to leverage that record. In fact, I've helped several clients navigate through this exact situation.

As you can see, performance evaluations are a valuable tool for both employees and organizations, but to make them serve *you*, you have to get strategic. For most underrepresented professionals, performance reviews can be some of the most difficult or frustrating experiences of their professional lives. If your leaders don't handle them correctly, they can scare you—like Ben's review did to Shay. If you've ever been blindsided in a performance review, you know how challenging it can be to regain the trust needed to operate at your full potential again and rebuild a positive narrative around your work. This is especially true for professionals of color.

Unless you are already known as a rock star and consistently affirmed through incredible feedback, performance evaluations are likely to feel heavy, difficult, and spark feelings of anxiety. Trying to compile all the good work you've done over long stretches of time, finding the balance of taking ownership of your contributions without sounding arrogant, and navigating the energy, temperament, and viewpoint of your manager feels like a process you simply have to survive through. The good news is, you can shift this experience by applying a few strategies in your conversations with your manager throughout the year to ensure you are protected and avoid being blindsided when it's time for performance and career conversations. With the right planning and preparation, you can make performance evaluations work for you, not against you.

Here's how to begin.

CAREER CHECK-INS

Career check-ins are thirty- to forty-five-minute conversations between you and your manager during which the conversation is completely focused on your career development. This differs from regular one-to-one meetings where you are responsible for briefing your leader on major projects and initiatives you're working on, as well as presenting your wins and requests.

During a career check-in, your leader should not ask you about status updates on work priorities, but rather keep the focus on your career goals and desires, and what you need to do to eventually attain these goals. This conversation should be about you, and *only* you.

I suggest scheduling a career check with your manager every eight to twelve weeks. (If your company has a performance evaluation quarterly, you may need to increase the regularity of the conversation to every six weeks.) The goal is to leave enough time between meetings for you to work toward feedback and gain examples of the results you've driven. If your career check-ins are too frequent, you may not have anything concrete to show your manager and the meetings may start to feel redundant for you both.

When approaching your manager about creating career check-in meetings, it's important to set expectations. These are not simply additional one-to-one meetings. The goal is to focus the time completely on discussing your career goals, key performance indicators that will help you meet your goals, and where you ultimately stand when it comes to performance and access to opportunities.

Regular career check-ins are a must because:

1). *You will always know where you stand.* If the goalposts keep moving (meaning, your manager keeps changing what you need to prove for promotion, higher compensation, other rewards, or how to get off a performance plan that could impact your employment), you can use these meetings to address the lack of clarity and use the techniques from earlier chapters (like follow-up emails and tracking your wins in your one-to-ones) to begin to lay the groundwork for your upward trajectory.

2). *You can avoid being blindsided in performance evaluations.* Career check-ins offer consistent conversations around development areas. Knowing this will allow you to work toward the feedback your manager gives you *before* you get into performance evaluation cycles.

3). *You're able to drive momentum.* When you limit career conversations to when your company tells you it's time to have them, you are indirectly agreeing to keep career conversations to a minimum. Therefore, unless your manager is proactively thinking about your promotion (which most, sadly, do not), you are likely to remain stagnant despite your great performance. Career check-ins allow you to create consistent yet comfortable accountability with your leaders, and also communicates that you do not intend to forget about the previous career conversations you've had.

When you decide to take control of your career conversations, you will realize that you can make them work for your benefit and receive what you desire—with the right planning. Starting these conversations several months before company-wide reviews will ensure your evaluation, and your case for career advancement, is successful.

The five steps to implementing powerful career check-in conversations are:

- Step 1: Scheduling and Alignment
- Step 2: Preparation and Engagement
- Step 3: Driving Momentum
- Step 4: Tracking and Reinforcing
- Step 5: Translating Results to Performance Evaluations

Let's look at each of these steps individually.

Step 1: Scheduling and Alignment

The first step toward successful career check-ins is presenting your ask to your manager (and other leaders), aligning on the proper cadence and timing of these meetings, and setting expectation for the meetings. Remember, you do not want to leave the door open for your manager to treat this conversation like your standard weekly one-to-one. Treat this as sacred space for your career development and set boundaries accordingly.

If you're feeling intimidated by setting such expectations with your leader, here is an email template you can leverage to request a regular career check-in:

> *Hi, [insert manager's name],*
>
> *I have been thinking strategically about my career here at [insert company name]. As you know, my desire is to grow within the company and continuously develop my skills to be*

a consistent contributor to our teams. I'd like to request your partnership as I explore and work toward development and advancement opportunities while also creating an environment for consistent performance feedback to ensure I'm on the right track.

Would you be open to having a career check-in conversation with me for thirty minutes every eight to twelve weeks? This would differ from our typical one-to-one as I'd like to keep the time completely focused on discussing my career goals and any feedback you may have for me that will help me reach my goals. For the first conversation, I'd like to discuss some of my overall career goals and receive your feedback on ways I can move the needle toward meeting those goals. Then, we can touch base every eight to twelve weeks as stated to see how I'm tracking.

If you are open to this, please let me know if it's okay to send you a standing calendar invite. I will also send you agenda items and questions in advance of these meetings, so we're aligned.

I'm happy to talk more about this in our next one-to-one. Thank you for your support and partnership.

[Your signoff]

Using this template, you have successfully made the ask, provided options for how regularly you'd like to meet, and set the expectation that this conversation should be about your development and advancement. You've also shown your commitment to making the discussions proactive by offering to send agenda topics and questions before every meeting. Most managers, if they are good leaders, will be thrilled to see this type of proactive and thoughtful approach to career development. It shows them that you don't feel you are entitled to rewards and incentives, but rather that you want to set goals and collaborate together to achieve them while continuing to invest in the company as a strong performer.

If you get pushback from your manager, I encourage you to take an inventory of what that says about your future within this team and about working with that leader. Leaders are put in position to help their direct reports grow and succeed within the company, and to retain top talent. It's okay if your manager prefers longer stretches of time between meetings (i.e., every sixteen weeks instead of every eight to twelve), as this may be more aligned with their schedule and responsibilities. However, if they flat-out refuse to grant you this much-deserved conversation, or give you a cop-out answer like, "I can't because this wouldn't be fair to your peers," I highly encourage you to consider a transition to another team, or another company. A leader's actions will always show you where you stand in a company and how far you will go under the leadership of this individual. Refusal or pushback tells you that this leader is lazy, hasn't bought into your value, or lacks key management skills. Knowing this sooner rather than later will save you the disappointment of working hard for months or years and getting nowhere.

When your manager agrees to these check-ins with you, take quick action. Thank them for their support, ask them what days and times they would prefer to have these check-ins, and send an invite that will reoccur on your calendar and theirs. This way, you know that a time slot is reserved for you every eight to twelve weeks (or whatever frequency you've agreed upon). I also encourage you to set a reminder on your own calendar a week before each career check-in to remind yourself to prepare, send agenda topics, and formulate questions so you can have a productive conversation.

Step 2: Preparation and Engagement

Now that you have a regular check-in on the calendar, you will create and send your agenda and questions five to seven days before the meeting. This will give your manager time to review your agenda and get answers to questions if they do not know them for themselves. Preparing your manager by staying organized is important. You want to help them help you.

Your first career conversation should cover the big picture of your career goals and how you'd like to grow within the company. This could be promotion, building a case for salary increase, developing specific skill sets, gaining access to work on higher visibility projects, and anything else that is top-of-mind for you. Then, you can share how you believe you've made progress toward those goals so far. You should also highlight how you've helped make progress toward company and team goals specifically, because no matter what your personal goals are, your manager likely cares about company and team initiatives more than anything else. Aligning your accomplishments to your organization's objectives and priorities will always resonate with decision-makers.

Next, ask your manager, "What is your feedback on what I've shared? In your opinion, am I on track to meet the career goals and benchmarks we've been talking about?" At this point your leader will tell you if you are on track or not.

If you are on track, you can say, "That's great to hear! What areas would you like for me to continue highlighting until our next career check-ins to prove I'm ready for [insert goal or desired outcome you communicated]? What are the next steps for me to potentially receive what I've been working toward?"

Asking these clear and concise questions will help you understand exactly where you stand, as well as the timeline of when you can expect to receive your request.

On the other hand, if you get constructive or negative feedback and your manager says you're not on track for your career goals and desired outcomes, don't be disheartened. Knowing the reality of your current position is the exact point of these check-ins. Acknowledge your manager's feedback and ask for suggestions on what you can do to improve. Then, share some ideas and ask them for their opinion on those ideas. If you do not agree with their feedback, thank them for bringing these items to your attention. Then, say, "Are you open to hearing some context on the feedback you provided?" and share your perspective, as well as any background information or miscommunications that could be driving their opinion. Maybe your context will help clear up misunderstandings or miscommunications, maybe not. Maybe your leader will be receptive, maybe not. Whatever the case, stay positive. The goal here is to keep dialogue open, even if that means agreeing to disagree.

There have been several occasions where I didn't agree with my leaders, and they knew it. I remember a leader citing "weak communication" as an area to work on. However, my communication wasn't weak. I just didn't communicate the way she preferred. She liked to text and send messages to me over Teams chat, but I liked to communicate via email so that the conversation was tracked and I could stay on top of next steps. The real problem was that she wasn't good on email. She would read them and forget to reply, and could never find emails she needed to refer to. So, in her view, my communication was weak. I didn't agree with her feedback, but it also wasn't worth the energy to explain my perspective. I learned quickly in my career to choose my battles, and this minor thing wasn't one. I simply chose to be mindful of prioritizing her texts and messages on Teams and then taking and filing screenshots of any items I wanted to create a record of. This was an annoying situation, but this manager and I were still able to have a good relationship.

Receiving feedback you don't agree with—and then having to prove to your manager that you've improved—isn't easy on your self-worth or confidence. I have felt challenged and angry about such situations, but deep inside, I knew that I couldn't hate the game if I wanted to succeed. Instead, I needed to play it. If you desire to stay within your team or company, it will be important for you to show your manager that you care about the feedback given, and will work on it. By asking, "What do you need to see from me that will turn this feedback around?" you're not admitting that you're in the wrong, only that you're listening and are mature enough to alleviate the challenge even if you don't agree. On the other hand, if you and your leader are completely misaligned and you have no desire to stay within the team, this will give you confirmation that it's time to move on and take steps toward your next journey—and that's not a bad place to be.

My desire for you is to always be informed and empowered to make decisions that serve you, even if they lead you down a path you didn't anticipate. You have more options than you think!

Step 3: Driving Momentum

Each career check-in should build on top of the one before. As mentioned, the first check-in is to clearly communicate your career goals and receive your manager's feedback. After you receive that feedback, you will know what you need to continuously showcase in your one-to-one's and future career check-ins. So, in your second career check-in, you should be delivering updates on how you've acted on the feedback given in the last check-in. The goal is to continuously communicate, receive feedback, communicate some more, and build a case for that development or advancement you're seeking. The conversation should continuously evolve until you receive what you're asking for. (We'll cover the negotiation process in the next chapter.)

However, a reminder: beware of the constantly moving goalposts. More often than not, managers will offer different or even contradictory direction on how you can achieve advancement, opportunities, and rewards. Just when you think you've proved what you needed to, they'll hand off another list of benchmarks you'll need to meet before your needs and desires can be met. This isn't fair to you, and I don't endorse wasting your time in these situations. Instead, address it right away by saying, "In the last several check-ins, you mentioned that if I proved success in A, B, and C, I would be on track for the [promotion, salary increase, seniority level increase] I have been working toward. However, now I'm hearing you say you need to see me prove D, E, and F. I'm confused with the shift in direction because I have been very intentional about following your feedback over the last several months to achieve this goal. Has something changed, and can you share more context?"

At this point, you're addressing the issue head-on. This sets the tone that you will keep your manager accountable for the feedback they give you. They may give you valid insight you didn't expect, for example, changes and shifts in direction within the organization that have not been communicated to the full team yet.

Such changes happen, and it could be more difficult for your manager to maneuver than you realize. However, be aware of behaviors. You'll know if your leaders are being truthful and supportive of your growth, or if they are simply stringing you along. Honest and empathetic leaders provide transparency and always keep you in the loop, even when situations are out of their control. They will honor your time and investment by providing you with the truth, clarity, next steps, and even share the areas where they don't have answers but are working on a resolution. Leaders who are stringing you along will never have an explanation. Instead, they will give you very vague explanations about why what they said before suddenly doesn't stand—and it will usually happen the moment you come close to meeting the bar and asking for what you want.

I like to remind my clients, "Trust your spirit." Your "spirit" is that tiny voice in your head, your heart, and your gut that tells you when something is off. You will always know someone's intentions by evaluating their actions. Do their actions back up their words? Pay close attention. It'll save you a ton of time, effort, and energy.

Step 4: Tracking and Reinforcing

After each career check-in, send a recap email immediately. Do not wait until the next day; you want to minimize the space for miscommunication or forgetting. While the meeting is fresh in your mind, recap what was discussed and the feedback that was given to you. Then, include a clear outline of next steps to keep both yourself and your leader accountable.

Here's an example recap email you can use to craft your own:

Hi, [insert manager's name],

Thank you, as always, for the career check-in conversation today. I'm grateful for the opportunity to discuss my career on a consistent basis, and I appreciate your support.

Today, we continued to discuss the plan we created for my promotion. In our last check-in, you shared that you'd like to see me prove examples of A, B, and C. Today I shared the following examples of how I've driven success in these areas including:

- *A [success examples]*
- *B [success examples]*
- *C [success examples]*

I was glad that you were pleased with these examples.

Today, you shared that you want me to compile examples of how I'm ready to deliver in the scope of my new role when I'm promoted. As a next step, I will work on getting that together and will share this with you in our next one-to-one.

I look forward to keeping the conversation going. If there is anything I've missed, please let me know.

Thank you again for your support.
[Your signoff]

An email like this recaps very clearly what was discussed, what was promised, and next steps, and invites your manager to add anything that you may have missed. Most importantly, it shows that you are following direction.

The recap is also rooted in gratitude, and provides a trail others can follow. If your manager abruptly leaves the organization, or if there is a re-org and you get a new manager, you can share your most recent recap email and pick up the conversation where you left off instead of having to start from scratch.

Where most people go wrong when discussing career is that they receive their manager's feedback and promises, but then have nothing to show for it because it was all verbal. If anything changes in the organization, the hard work you've put into driving strategic career conversations could be in jeopardy.

You need to protect the hard work you're putting into your advancement and development. Verbal agreements mean nothing. Even if it feels uncomfortable, nobody else can protect your efforts. It's up to you. The post-conversation email recap enables you to record and track what is discussed over time.

Step 5: Translating into Performance Evaluations

At this point, you know the strategy to drive powerful career conversations through the Brij the Gap One-to-One Meeting Agenda and the career check-in formula. The Brij the Gap Agenda template will allow you to leverage your one-to-one meetings with your leaders to not only discuss priorities, but also to drive visibility toward your contributions and accomplishments. The career check-in conversations enable you to make your career goals and desires known and have a plan that involves your leader (and other decision-makers) to consistently move the needle toward the success you're seeking.

These conversations are incredibly important on their own, but it's also important to translate the key points from both into formal, company-wide performance evaluations. Why? Because this evaluation is typically tracked in your company's HRIS (Human Resources Information System) and therefore has the most visibility of any documentation around your success and value. Human Resources, future hiring managers (if you're applying for an internal role), and other leaders can access these reports to get a picture of how you've performed. It's typically the first place decision-makers will go to see if you are actually a key contributor for the company.

Because so many eyeballs are on performance evaluations, it's critical for you to make sure the important topics you've been discussing in your weekly one-to-one's and career check-ins make it into these official documents.

So, how do you do that? By leveraging your one-to-one agenda template according to the range of time covered by the performance evaluation, and gathering positive feedback from your one-to-ones, career check-ins, and also from your career allies, sponsors, and mentors.

Begin by leveraging the Brij the Gap One-to-One Meeting Agenda template I shared in Chapter Nine. Because you have already recorded your wins, inform, discuss, and ask items into a spreadsheet, you will be able to easily filter out what you need for your self-assessment. Also, pull up the agendas and recap emails you've shared from previous career check-in conversations to get a full picture of how you're driving success for your teams, the overall company, and your clients or stakeholders.

When gathering information for your performance evaluation, consider the range of time being measured. Is the company assessing the last six months (typically called a mid-year review), the past quarter (quarterly review), or the past year (annual review)? Again, all you have to do is go back to your one-to-one agenda template and filter out the wins, inform, and discuss sections for that particular time frame. You'll then have a complete view of every single thing you're proud about and worked on. Can I get an amen? Talk about a huge weight off your shoulders! Another bonus is, because you've shared these examples in the past, your manager's memory will be refreshed on how you've been showing up consistently.

Once you've got all the examples of your accomplishments and wins at hand, choose the strongest examples to include in your performance evaluation. Your company may already have a preexisting set of questions about particular strengths or how you're driving toward their culture and values. You can easily answer these by selecting examples from the list you've compiled from your agenda and email records. Don't be shy; instead, be thorough. It's your responsibility to ensure your examples are both clear and concise.

Here's the thing most people don't realize. Performance evaluations should *not* be the first time your manager and other leaders gain visibility into your contributions, your accomplishments, your wins, and your goals for advancement. Rather, performance evaluations should be opportunities to recap, reiterate, and remind your leaders of your great work, and to continuously position yourself to be seen as a consistent driver toward team and company success. This makes it a no-brainer to select you over others for opportunities, incentives, and rewards.

PERFORMANCE REVIEW ETIQUETTE

Now that you've got the preparation part of your performance evaluations all set, it will be easier to step confidently into this important conversation. I've taught you to execute powerfully—but remember, this conversation is also an opportunity to hear from your leader and gain constructive feedback. No matter how iron-clad your wins and metrics, you need to leave room for your manager to say their piece. Remember, you may or may not agree with what they say, but hopefully, given your powerful and effective one-to-one meetings and consistent career check-ins, you won't be blindsided by anything. Of course, I can't promise this will be the case, particularly if you are working with a manager who has been combative or shown signs that they aren't interested in your growth, and in general you should always be prepared for the unexpected. Whatever happens, though, you will go into this process knowing that you have done everything you could to position yourself for success.

Here are a few more key tips for successfully navigating your performance evaluations:

- *Be on time.* That sounds obvious, right? However, it's common for people to be unintentionally late for their review. This in turn communicates that you aren't serious about your career or respectful of your leader. So, remove all barriers that could cause you to be late, including blocking your calendar for at least thirty minutes before your scheduled evaluation. Don't take any calls. Don't cut it close by trying to grab lunch at that super busy taco spot across the street. Give your team a head's up that you need to leave that meeting ten minutes early so you can be on time for your review. Planning ahead will ensure you show up on time and ready to go.

- *Be engaged.* Practice effective listening, maintain eye contact, and do not interrupt when your manager is speaking. You can also take notes as they deliver feedback, and reinforce that you are digesting their feedback through the occasional head nod.

- *Anticipate criticism or lack of affirmation.* Perhaps your manager doesn't think you're ready for that promotion. Maybe they aren't impressed with your accomplishments (although, hopefully, your one-to-ones and career check-ins will mitigate this). These things are normal. I've seen the highest achievers and performers experience criticisms and negative feedback in their reviews, too. The best thing you can do is maintain composure, breathe deeply, and try not to react in a negative way. When your leader finishes their thought, you can seek understanding by saying, "I'd like to understand that better," or, "Do you mind sharing more context? I'm a little confused by the example you shared." This basically tells your leader you don't agree, sets the expectation that they need to be thorough with their criticisms, and ensures you're not being viewed as "defensive" or "unable to take feedback." Hear their response, and then keep it moving. Dwelling on every criticism will not serve you well in this setting.

- *Show appreciation.* Thank your leader for the time they've invested in the conversation, even if you didn't agree with the feedback offered. Don't argue your point during the evaluation, no matter how tempting it might be. Remember, the goal is not to prove your manager wrong, but rather to be seen as a valuable, mature contributor to the team and company, and someone worth investing in. That perception will carry you farther than attempting to prove a point that will eventually become irrelevant.

- *Follow up appropriately.* If you felt blindsided by unexpected criticisms (whether you agree with them or not), ask for time to review them together in your next one-to-one or career check-in conversation. Over the week following your review, brainstorm potential solutions or ways to avoid those mistakes in the future, and share them with your manager. Your personal evaluation setting is not the environment to do that—such discussions should take place in a follow-up conversation—but this effort shows your leader that you take their feedback seriously.

When executed strategically, performance reviews can go from a dreaded and stressful experience to something that works for you. As we've discussed, there are plenty of situations you can't control, but also plenty where you have more power than you think. Taking the approach you learned in this chapter, start implementing the Brij the Gap Agenda in your one-to-one meetings and initiate consistent career check-ins every eight to twelve weeks (if you haven't already). This will set you up for successful career conversations in all capacities.

I promise you, this approach will ensure that not only do you feel empowered, but also that others view you as a powerful force within the company. You've got this!

Chapter Eleven

MASTERING NEGOTIATION

I MET ALIYAH several years ago when she enrolled in my four-week accelerator, Brij the Gap (then called BrandU). She was active, engaged, and truly immersed herself in the education and coaching resources I offered. By week four, her confidence levels when approaching career advancement was day and night compared to week one. She was invested in her success, and it was evident.

About a year later, I got an email from Aliyah asking if I could offer her one-to-one coaching. She was applying and actively interviewing for a role she really wanted. The role excited her, she liked the company, and the office was a quick fifteen-minute drive from her home. In short, it looked like the perfect role for her. Of course, I agreed to coach Aliyah through the interview process. Aliyah is bright, driven, and incredibly personable. I had no doubt—especially given the extra work she was doing to prepare for her multiple rounds of interviews—that she would get an offer.

A few weeks later, I got a call from Aliyah. "Devika, they made me an offer!"

"Yaaas! Congratulations!" I gushed, practically dancing with happiness for her. "What's the offer? Are you happy with it?"

"Well, it's for $65,000 a year, which is only $5,000 more than I'm currently making. I guess it's something, but I wanted more."

I felt my heart sink. Aliyah's potential contribution to this company was worth far more than that! "What was the range of pay they communicated to you?" I asked.

"$65,000 to $98,000."

"Okay, great. You're going to ask for $95,000."

Aliyah was silent.

"Does that number not align with what you want?" I asked.

"Of course it does, Devika. But how can I ask for *so* much more?"

"Have you disclosed the salary for your current position?"

"No."

"Okay, that's good. So, let's talk about how you can do this."

Aliyah was hesitant and scared. As much as she had grown and challenged herself in my accelerator, negotiation still felt intimidating.

I talked her through the fact that she wasn't asking for something they had not already budgeted for. Sure, asking for $95,000 instead of $65,000 seemed liked a stretch, but she was an incredibly strong candidate. She had the experience to warrant the $95,000 salary, and the role was much more senior than her current position.

After explaining this in detail, Aliyah embraced that she was worthy of that additional compensation, despite how uncomfortable it felt to make this ask. "After all," she said, "the worst they can say is no."

Together, we worked through the preparation and delivery of how to request a higher salary than the one stated in the offer letter. The next morning, I sent Aliyah a text message with a mini pep talk on why she deserved that compensation, and assured her that negotiations were simply a conversation. Even if they didn't give her the full $95,000, it was likely that they would meet her in the middle.

Later in the day, Aliyah called me. "What did they say?" I asked anxiously.

"They gave me $95,000!" I could hear the joy in her voice. This jump in salary would set a baseline that every employer in the future would have to build from. The best part, though, was that Aliyah would now be able to give her son, who is on the spectrum, access to out-of-pocket Autism therapy. I was beyond thrilled for her.

If Aliyah hadn't reached out to me for coaching, she would likely have taken the $65,000 salary without negotiating. After all, it was slightly more than her current pay—and isn't that better than nothing? My direct coaching helped Aliyah in this situation, but it also showed her that she didn't need me for every negotiation she would engage in in the future. In fact, she now had the formula and tools to respectfully but powerfully advocate for her needs with this and future employers.

In this chapter, I'm going to teach you the exact negotiation strategies I taught Aliyah.

WHY NEGOTIATE?

Negotiation. The word alone makes many underrepresented professionals cringe. In fact, most of us shy away from this experience altogether.

When you think of negotiation, you might envision an aggressive tennis match, trading offers and counteroffers, making threats and promises. It's painfully uncomfortable to endure. So instead, you just hope that decision-makers around you will acknowledge your value and offer fair and merit-based compensation, recognition, and rewards. Even if they don't, you're willing to take what you can get. After all, you should feel lucky to be at that company, in that role, making what you do. Most people would do anything to be in your position, right?

We tackled this mindset at the beginning of this book, but nowhere does it reemerge more strongly and in more debilitating ways than during a negotiation process. I'm here to tell you that gratitude and humility can exist simultaneously with ambition and wanting more for yourself.

I couldn't write a book about commanding the career you deserve without giving you the formula to master negotiation. Negotiation, after all, is a necessary process of getting you the income, resources, and opportunities you desire. Is it uncomfortable? Yes. Will it ever be entirely comfortable? Probably not. Even I don't feel entirely comfortable negotiating, and I do it every day as I create and refine contracts for the companies who hire me to support their employees and leaders. But guess what? I do it anyway—and powerfully, if I do say so myself—because I know the value I drive and understand precisely how to deliver what my clients need.

I've never once met a person of color who has said, "Devika, I am *completely confident* in my ability to negotiate for my salary, opportunities, and resources." *Not once.*

It's my mission to change this.

Why Are We So Afraid to Negotiate?

The discomfort, fear, and paralysis you may feel when going through a negotiation process didn't just pop up overnight. Like we discussed in earlier chapters, challenges around self-advocacy are rooted in your personal experiences, upbringing, culture, and the parameters around asking and receiving that have been reinforced in your life over time. People of color face unique challenges and fears related to negotiation in the workplace due to historical, cultural, and systemic factors.

Here are some examples of why you may struggle with negotiation in the workplace:

- *Fear of rejection.* You may fear that your requests will be denied or even ridiculed, leading you to feel embarrassed or discouraged.
- *Fear of retaliation.* You may fear that you will face negative consequences or be viewed unfavorably by your leadership teams if you ask for what you want and deserve.
- *Cultural upbringing.* In some cultures, there may be an emphasis on humility and respect for authority figures, which can discourage assertiveness in negotiations.
- *Stereotyping.* You may fear that being assertive or owning your value in negotiations will reinforce negative stereotypes or biases about your ethnic or racial group.

- *Language barriers.* For individuals whose first language is not English, language barriers can pose an additional challenge in negotiations, making it difficult for them to assert themselves effectively.

If any (or most) of these examples resonated with you, you're not alone. Most underrepresented professionals experience one or more of these factors with regard to negotiation. However, there are remedies that can minimize these fears and help you feel more confident when you come to the negotiating table.

Prepare, Prepare, Prepare

The first step in negotiation, like everything else, is preparation.

When most people approach negotiation, they think of what they want to ask for and quickly jump into making that ask of their leaders and decision-makers. However, this skips several critical steps.

Before you begin any negotiation, take an inventory of where you stand with your performance.

If you have the reputation of being a great performer, the feedback leadership has shared has been consistently glowing, and you have a strong and proven track record of success? Well, then you have the opportunity to ask for and receive what matters to you, including a great salary. I believe there is more within your reach than you have imagined, and it's time to go for it!

On the other hand, if you are not performing within expectations, or better yet exceeding expectations, now is *not* the time to ask for promotions, incentives, or rewards. Of course, if you want to negotiate resources that will help you perform better and strengthen your skills—like access to a coach, educational courses, and other tools—that's a different scenario. Vulnerably admitting you need extra help and asking for resources to do your job better shows you are committed to turning your reality around for the betterment of your career, your team, and your company. However, if you're seeking a salary increase, promotion, or access to higher-visibility projects but have not received feedback that you are in good standing with your leadership team, asking for rewards and recognition will not serve you well. Instead, focus your time on becoming a good performer and developing a reputation of being a solid contributor to the team. Leverage your career check-in conversations to develop a plan to get back on track and meet those milestones.

Know Your Options

When most people step into negotiations, they are only asking for one thing. Everything is riding on that one ask. They go to the decision-maker, make the request—and if they are denied, they slip away in defeat. They feel rejected and embarrassed, which discourages them from negotiating again. In fact, they may feel that, since they didn't get what they were asking for, their only option is to leave the team or company. Can you relate?

The best way to ensure a successful negotiation is to prepare multiple options that you would be happy to receive. This way, you're not pinning all of your hopes on one outcome. Just like good investors know that you cannot put all your money into one asset, but should instead diversify, great negotiators know that having multiple requests, fallbacks, and acceptable outcomes can ensure that everyone at the table gets at least some portion of what they want.

Your Career Brainstorm Chart

The Career Brainstorm Chart is something my clients use to get crystal clear about what they are actually seeking so they can be clear with their leaders.

Your manager, leaders, and other decision-makers are not mind readers. So, it's important to give them all of the information and context in order to understand exactly what you are seeking and make choices accordingly.

Let's say that, once you muster up the courage to kick off the negotiation conversation with your leader, you start by saying something like, "I'd like to get paid more." Well, you've left it up to your leader to determine what "more" is, and how much they want to give you. You need to define exactly what "more money" means to you, and have several alternatives defined and ready to share in case your first request cannot be fulfilled.

So, let's put that together in the Career Brainstorm Chart.

Career Desire: ______________________	
What you're asking for	**How that could look**
Option #1	• Option #1-a • Option #1-b • Option #1-c
Option #2	• Option #2-a • Option #2-b • Option #2-c
Option #3	• Option #3-a • Option #3-b • Option #3-c

In the top row, you will highlight your career desire. Then, in the two columns, you will outline what you're asking for and what the end result could look like. You'll then use these criteria to identify exactly what you're asking for so there is no room for misunderstanding when you position your request to your leaders.

I'll share an example of how this works using the story of my client, Simone.

Simone's career desire was to receive better compensation for the value she was driving. She wrote this down in the "Career Desire" area of the chart. However, "better compensation" can look like several different things, so she needed to define what that meant. To her, better compensation could look like a promotion, monetary compensation, and/or the company investing leadership development resources into her. She jotted those down in the "What You're Asking For" column as options 1, 2, and 3.

Then, she took it a step further—and this is the part that most people miss. She went on to qualify what "promotion," "monetary compensation," and "leadership development" looked like for her.

"Promotion" could look like more opportunities to lead and a job title change to a senior level. "Monetary compensation" could look like a $10,000 annual increase, a one-time bonus of $10,000, or an $8,000 stipend that could be used to pay for a career coach and/or leadership courses she wanted to take to develop her skills.

For "leadership development," she wanted access to four key leadership conferences a year. She wanted the company to pay for those, and not require her to use vacation days to attend. She also wanted to be included in the company's internal "Rising Stars" program that helped train high-potential talent who desired to become people managers.

After identifying these asks, her chart looked like this:

Career Desire: ***Receive better compensation for the value I'm driving***	
What you're asking for	**How that could look**
Option #1: Promotion	• Opportunities to lead • Change job title to "senior"
Option #2: Monetary Compensation	• $10,000 salary increase • $10,000 annual bonus • $8,000 education/career development stipend
Option #3: Leadership Development	• Rising Stars program • Attend four paid confer-ences annually

Knowing all of this in advance, Simone could clearly communicate the end result she was seeking, avoid being vague with her manager, and show up stronger in her negotiations.

What Options Should You Choose?

As I mentioned before, most people make the mistake of having only one option to present to decision-makers when entering a negotiation. If the decision-maker is unable to accommodate that request, they're left with nothing to fall back on. They may also feel rejected and undervalued, which can negatively affect their confidence in future negotiations.

In a perfect world, the person you're negotiating with would say, "I can't accommodate that, but I can look into providing this instead." However, this rarely happens in practice—especially if you are renegotiating your existing role, compensation, or access to opportunities. If you're negotiating a new role and compensation, you may have a better chance of that response—but still, it's rare. In none of the above cases does this automatically mean that the decision-maker doesn't want to help you consider alternative options. It's just that, most of the time, people tend to only evaluate what is being communicated to them. Therefore, it's important for *you* to drive that conversation.

My success in negotiating has always come from presenting three options, starting with the one I desire most. If the decision-maker rejects the first option, I present the next. If I still don't get a yes, I have one more option in my back pocket to ask for. More often than not, using this strategy, I end up receiving at least something I asked for between the first and third options I presented.

To create your options, first refer to the "How That Could Look" column of your career brainstorm chart. Taking the examples you included, create three options: your ideal option (option A), your exceptional option (option B), and your great option (option C).

Your ideal option should be your picture-perfect scenario. In this season of your career, if you could have this *one thing*, you would feel like jumping for joy. Option A should be an uncomfortable ask—as though you're shooting for just a little (or a lot) too much. (I promise, you're not asking for too much, but the critical voice in your head will make you believe you are.)

Your exceptional option (B) is something you would still be incredibly happy to receive, but is less of an ask than your ideal option. Your great option (C) is something you would also be happy to receive, but is an even more minor ask than your exceptional option.

Notice that you would be happy to receive any of the three options you've identified. If what you're asking for and including in option A, B, or C feels like you're compromising on a component of feeling rewarded and recognized the way you'd like, don't bother including it. You're not here to settle. You're here to win, and stay winning, as you move from season to season in your career.

Taking Simone's chart as an example, let's walk through how to put together your options. In the "How That Could Look" column, Simone identified:

- Opportunities to lead
- Job title change to "senior"
- $10,000 salary increase annually
- $10,000 annual bonus
- $8,000 in educational or coaching stipend
- Access to the Rising Stars program
- Access to four paid leadership conferences a year

Taking this information, Simone organized and ranked her desires under option A (ideal), option B (exceptional), and option C (great) in the chart.

Creating these options helped Simone understand what truly mattered to her when negotiating with her manager, instead of simply asking for vague outcomes like "advancement" or "promotion." There would have been room for her manager to misinterpret "advancement" and "promotion" and what that meant to Simone, but making a precise ask like "Senior title, $10,000 salary increase, and access to participate in Rising Stars" could not be misunderstood.

Do you see how she transformed her career goals and desires from "receive better compensation for the value I'm driving" to the actual details of what she wanted? With specific asks in hand, her leader could figure out what was doable and what was not.

The same will be true for you if you follow the strategies I've presented.

MAKING THE ASK

Now that you have Options A, B, and C clearly outlined, it's time to make your request through negotiating with your manager.

First, you want to request Option A, your ideal option. Remember, it may feel like you're asking for way too much, but you're not. If your manager pushes back or says they cannot accommodate, then, instead of retreating or stopping the negotiation altogether, you'll ask if they will consider Option B, your exceptional option. If they cannot accommodate those requests, that's when you can make your final request for them to consider Option C, your great option.

Seems like a lengthy process, right? It is, and it isn't. If you can't wrap your head around an ask of that length or complexity, I guarantee that you're in for a surprise. This is how negotiation goes. You just need to embrace the discomfort and show up confidently despite it.

What typically happens between Options A, B, or C is that your manager will be able to say an immediate yes to at least one of your asks, or even present an alternative option that may satisfy you. If you've exhausted your options and your leader isn't able to accommodate anything (and they aren't making any suggestion of what they could offer you, or when they might be able to meet your requests down the road), you will need to make a decision to stay or go. Recalling my initial point around getting real with where you stand: if you know you have a great reputation and are known as an asset to your team and company, your managers will likely try to give you something to appease you because they want to keep you on the team. Often, leaders would love to be able to give you your Option A and make you happy, but there are factors outside of their control (like budget cuts and freezes, change in upper management, upcoming shifts in the organization they can't communicate yet, etc.), that hinder their ability to give you what you want. It's nothing personal, just the reality of the challenges they have to work through as a leader. Hopefully in these cases, they will let you know what's going on to respect your time, effort, and energy, and manage your expectations. However, even if their inability to meet your asks is out of your manager's control, it's up to you whether you want to stick around and wait for your desires to be delivered or move on to another company that will compensate and recognize you as you deserve. There's no right or wrong answer. You have to follow your gut and trust yourself as you evaluate situations and make decisions that best serve you. You'll know by the actions of your leaders if they truly want to recognize and incentivize you to stay. If the goalposts are consistently moving or you're met with empty promises month after month, this is a clear indicator it's time to go somewhere where you will be valued. Or, if you feel that you are valued and that your leaders truly are working toward giving you what you need, it's okay to trust them and be patient.

I've been in situations where friends and peers were encouraging me to leave a company because the promotion or salary increase I requested was taking too long. They felt that, as a woman of color,

I should boldly stand my ground and demand what I wanted—and if decision-makers weren't budging, it was time to walk away to prove my point. However, I knew in these cases that my manager was actively having conversations about my advancement and growth. It was just taking her longer than anticipated because she had to navigate upper management and HR to get them to sign off on what I wanted. Would leaving to prove a point have served me? Not in those cases.

The Full Cycle of Negotiation

In this section, I'll take you through the full cycle of negotiations with your manager after you have prepared and organized your ideal, exceptional, and great options.

Here's how I coached Simone to approach her manager, John:

- Simone: *John, thank you for taking the time to meet with me today. As you know, we've been having many discussions about my future here. It's been great to know that you and the leadership team view me as a strong contributor to the team. I love being here and want to continue growing within the company. I'd like to open up a discussion about my compensation. I've been reflecting on my role here and the contributions I've made over the last two years. I'm glad we both agree that I've taken on more responsibilities and that I've consistently delivered results beyond the responsibilities of this role. We've discussed examples to prove these points in my career check-in conversations and the fact that I have not received a salary increase in the two years that I've been here. I think it's a fair time to revisit compensation and I had a few requests I'd like to present for consideration if you're open to it.*

- John: *I appreciate your hard work and dedication to the team. What do you have in mind?*

- Simone: *We've had conversations in the past about raising my compensation. I've expressed that I believe my offer was on the lower end for this role, especially compared to my experience. In the two years I've been here, I've received consistent feedback that I've exceeded expectations and that good work is why I'm selected to take on higher-visibility initiatives. Because of that, along with the fact that I have not received a salary increase or bonus over the typical threshold, I'd like to ask for a $10,000 annual raise. Given my performance and market conditions, I believe this is a fair adjustment to industry standards. Additionally, I'd like to request that my title be changed to reflect "Senior," given I take on the highest-priority initiatives across the team. Lastly, I'd like to be considered for the Rising Stars program because it will provide me with the coaching I need to move into a people manager role in the future. I know we've talked about my desire to move into a management role in the next year. What is your feedback on these requests?*

- John: *Thank you for being clear about what you need to see. I'll consult with the senior leadership and HR teams to see what can be accommodated to ensure we're aligning with company policy.*

- Simone: *I understand. Thanks for advocating for me, John. When is a good time for us to follow up on this conversation?*
- John: *Give me a week or so. Let me see what we can do and come back to you.*

Unfortunately, John came back a week later with some not-so-great news.

- John: *Simone, as you know, the company is looking to make cuts to budget given the uncertainty of the economy. Unfortunately, I can't meet your expectations for a $10,000 increase, but given your experience and benchmarks for the role, I can offer you an additional $5,000 in annual compensation.*
- Simone: *I'm disheartened to hear that because, as I look to grow within the company, feeling like I'm being compensated for work that consistently exceeds expectations is a big part. Would the leadership team be open to meeting me in the middle at a $7,500 increase, and a one-time bonus of $5,000? Also, was there any feedback on me being selected for Rising Stars?*

John didn't have the immediate answer, so he had to go back to the HR and leadership teams again. A few days later, he offered Simone a $7,500 annual increase, a $3,000 bonus (on top of her current bonus), and submitted her for the Rising Stars program.

Was it exactly her ideal option? No. But she got her key ask of being included in the program, and her salary increase and extra bonus added up to the $10,000 she asked for, even though it wasn't in the exact form she expected. More, John was willing to meet her where she was, even though he couldn't give her exactly what she asked for. All of these factors made Simone happy. She didn't even need to position her Option C because she was successful in her negotiation by the second conversation. Also, the experience showed her that John did honor her contribution to the team and was willing to advocate for her. If he had given her a flat-out no without exploring options, that would have been her cue to start looking for a role outside the company.

My point in sharing this exchange is to show you a few key things:

- You need to be crystal clear about what you're asking for by providing examples, amounts, and all details. Vague statements like "higher compensation" will not cut it.
- Do not be intimidated by the fact that you may need to have multiple conversations before you get what you need. As long as you are composed, respectful, and allow your manager the space to advocate for you, you will not be seen in a negative light.
- It's important to hear what your manager is saying when they present feedback. John stated that the company was making financial cuts, so asking for the higher bonus or education stipends which Simone included in her original Options B and C would have shown that she wasn't listening to the feedback. She had her exceptional and great options prepared, but

she pivoted accordingly while staying true to what she wanted, based on John's feedback.

You may be asking, "Devika, what if I'm negotiating a new job offer at a new company?"

If that's the case, I want you to take the same approach in positioning your ask, and take some additional steps to ensure they see your worth and are willing to compensate you fairly as a result. Here is how to apply this strategy to negotiating an external job offer:

- *Do your research.* Know the typical salary range for the position in your industry and location. You can Google online salary surveys, calculators, and job postings to get a general sense of the range. Several states have salary transparency laws that require employers to provide salary range information to applicants, specifically through job postings, which can be helpful. However, the downside is that the ranges provided are huge and, therefore, hard to navigate. I recently saw a job posting with the salary range reflecting $65,000 – $175,000. In talking with HR professionals and executives in my network, they've explained that by broadening the range, they're able to look at a variety of candidates with differing experiences and tenure. The key, no matter what, is for you to determine your worth in the market and do your research so that when you disclose your salary expectations, you're leading with data that makes a strong case for your request.

- *Understand what you want.* Create your Options A, B, and C, and introduce each option to the recruiter or hiring manager one at a time until you come to an agreement you're excited about.
- *Don't be afraid to have the recruiter make your requests known to the hiring manager*—even if they need to go back several times. This is a common experience for recruiters, and what may feel highly uncomfortable for you is simply part of their job.
- *Make sure you are happy with your offer.* Every salary increase in future will be based on that offer. It's important for you to get the number and benefits you're seeking from the very beginning. (That's why I pushed Aliyah to ask for the most she possibly could get.) As a candidate that the company wanted to hire, she had the most power in that moment to get what she wanted.
- *When asked about salary expectations, flip the question.* You can say, "One of the questions I had was regarding the pay range for this role. Can you disclose the range for this position?" Most recruiters at this point will disclose the range, but if they flip the question right back to you, provide your expected salary range versus a firm number (based on your research of what you could ask for).
- *If you can, buy time.* Remember, once you've put a number out there, you're going to be held to that

number (or range). By the time you get to the end of the interview process and are a final candidate, you might have learned more about what will be required of you, which can affect your desired compensation. If you've stated a number early on, you won't be able to backtrack seamlessly. So, if you can swing it, buy time by saying something like, "Can we wait until later in the process to discuss pay? There are so many elements like base pay, bonuses, and benefits at play, and I'd really like to spend the time deserved for this if I'm one of your final candidates." This response will help keep you in the running, moving forward with the process without undercutting yourself. If this isn't possible, and the recruiter is persistent, have your pay range (based on research) prepared.

- *Don't be afraid to ask for more.* Negotiating with a new company where you're not yet connected to the leaders feels less intimidating, so go for it! It's very unlikely that you'll lose an offer unless you're being unreasonable. Companies expect you to negotiate. I can tell you from my Human Resources days that companies usually buffer in additional compensation, perks, and benefits for those who don't take the first offer. Negotiation, when done with composure and grace, is typically well-received in the offer stage of the hiring process. Showing that you know your worth and are willing to work to receive what you need shows you're a strong employee, not a weak one.

If you're negotiating an offer with a new company, here are a few more things I want you to do differently than someone who is negotiating within their existing company and/or team:

- *Proactively prove your credibility.* Ask three to five previous colleagues, managers, or clients to write you a recommendation on LinkedIn. (Recommendations allow people to highlight your work or how they enjoyed working with you.) When a recruiter or hiring manager sees this, they will feel more confident hiring you and are often willing to increase their budget to secure you as an employee. Often, people ask, "Why do I need to do this if they're going to ask for referrals anyway?" Referral checks are a standard part of the process to ensure you are being truthful about your employment. While hiring managers may ask for feedback on your performance or ability to be a team player, referral checks are more about uncovering any red flags than determining your credibility. Having multiple LinkedIn recommendations is a proactive way to showcase that you're a safe and worthy person to hire. Do your best not to make recruiters and hiring managers fish for your testimonials; instead, provide them with what they need to extend an offer that exceeds your expectations.
- *Ensure alignment.* Make sure that your resume and any examples of work you share in the interview process align to the job description. What skills are they looking for? What can you share that proves

you know how to drive the end result? How have you solved problems similar to what they are currently challenged with? As you update your resume or prepare for your interviews, the job description should be your main reference point. Often, people get caught up in sharing their successes in previous roles, but if those successes aren't relevant to the role you're applying for, it can feel like a distraction to your interview panel.

- *Use your executive summary.* Your executive summary can be leveraged to showcase your contributions and value. Feel free to share it with your recruiter and/or your interview panel. The executive summary can help you highlight specific results and strengths that may get missed on a wordy resume.
- *Use the STAR method (below) when explaining your accomplishments.* The STAR method helps to provide the complete context and result of your accomplishments, making you a desired candidate.
    - *Set the scene*: Provide brief context on what the situation was before you were able to contribute to solving the challenge or driving a positive result.
    - *Tasks:* Explain how you took on specific tasks to help drive the solution.
    - *Action:* Explain the actions you took, including challenges you experienced and how you worked through them to deliver a positive end result.

- *Result:* Clearly highlight the positive outcome of your accomplishment and the impact you made to others involved.

Here's an example of how to use the STAR method in your response during an interview:

One accomplishment I'm proud of is retaining a high-priority client and saving Company XYZ over $500,000 in revenue. My team was experiencing high turnover over the course of the last year and my peer, who originally managed this account, abruptly left the company. This caused a lot of stress on the leadership team and anxiety for the client, so I offered to step into the role until my manager could find a replacement to manage the account.

I quickly introduced myself to the client and their team, assured them that I was here to help maintain consistency in the support they needed, and that I was committed to their success. I also kept my leadership team updated and asked for help when needed to ensure a seamless experience for the client. Using the notes that were in the system, I created and introduced a project plan that would help deliver the client's goals. I was able to help the client meet their desired result while empathetically supporting them through this unexpected change.

The result was that we retained the client rather than losing them to a competitor; this preserved $500,000 in revenue that was at risk. One of my personal values is honoring relationships and acting like an owner when my team is in need, so I was grateful to contribute in this way.

Answering like this shows your interview panel that you not only care about your job and values, but also the overall success of your team, company, and other stakeholders. Employers are happy to invest in candidates like that!

By following these steps in addition to the central negotiation strategy of presenting your Options A, B, and C, you will be in a solid position to effectively negotiate.

***

Negotiating for your advancement may never feel comfortable, but as long as you follow through with the methods I've taught you, you'll always end up in a better position than you started. Through my own experience, Simone's and Aliyah's experiences, or the experiences of the thousands of other underrepresented professionals I've coached, I've seen over and over that pushing through your discomfort around negotiation will bring you a blessing on the other side. I can't promise that your negotiations will always work completely in your favor, but I *can* tell you that you will always be positioned to make empowered decisions for yourself if you employ the strategies you learned in the last several chapters.

So, embrace the discomfort, follow the strategies, pay attention to how your proposal is being received, and make decisions according to what your spirit, heart, and gut are telling you.

I'm so excited to see you shine.

Chapter Twelve

YOUR EXIT STRATEGY

"YOU'RE NOT A FIT for this company."

After nearly five years of working at a company I loved, building my personal brand, fostering relationships with colleagues and leaders across North America, and successfully performing in each of the three positions I held during my tenure, this comment … well, it hurt. A lot. Rather than feedback on my performance, this was an attack on my values and integrity, and it cut deeply.

It was worse that these words were spoken by Heather, who had only managed me for a few months at that point. How could it be that leaders I'd worked with in the past saw me as a clear asset to the team and company, yet Heather was so comfortable telling me she didn't want me around?

For the four months leading up to that comment, I felt like I was in hell almost every day. My experience in the workplace before I had taken on this new, more senior role within another organization felt like a gift. Sure, there were challenges, but I truly loved going to work every day, engaging with my colleagues, and working with my clients. But this new role and the team culture (or lack thereof) felt like an abrupt shift, even though I hadn't changed companies. The decline of my and Heather's relationship, which had started so strong, began with feedback from another colleague whom I introduced in earlier chapters, Shannon.

Shannon was a senior sales representative with whom I partnered on client accounts. She was from a tiny town in Georgia, and had a heavy Southern accent, which she liked to play up. She would just glow when people referred to her as a "Southern belle." She walked extra "hard" so everyone would notice the click-clack sounds of her red-bottom heels in client meetings. She loved talking about her two-night trips to Europe, her weekends in the Hamptons, and her dinners at the trendiest restaurants. She may have come from Georgia, but she was a New Yorker now, and she made sure everyone knew it.

"Live your best life!" I would always say to her—because she seemed happy, and I was happy for her. But my God-given sense for people let me know early on that something was off. Shannon was nice to people's faces, but also had a low-key shade about her. As long as she wasn't shady with me, I didn't pay it too much attention—but then, one day, her entitled behavior became a personal attack on me.

Because the clients we worked with were our company's largest spenders and therefore highest priority, there were two account managers assigned to each client. Shannon was a level higher than me, owned more responsibility than me, and was paid significantly more as a result. Her actions showed that she felt that she had certain privileges I was not entitled to. It was acceptable for her to operate in certain ways, but not me. For example, Shannon would leave work for hours at a time to get her hair done without putting in for a half-day off, or even letting our manager know. She claimed to be "working from her phone"—but for someone who would swarm our team's inboxes all day and night, she was awfully quiet during those hair appointments. Shannon also had a boyfriend in Paris, the same city one of our clients was headquartered in. She would intentionally arrange frivolous meetings with the client (that could have been done virtually) to fly to Paris on the company's dime and extend her stay into the weekend to spend time with her boyfriend. On the other hand, if I started work an hour later than usual because my flight got in late the night before and I was exhausted in the morning, I was viewed as abusing our flexible work environment, and when I booked a few nights in New York City to have face time with our team, Shannon complained to our managers that the trips were unwarranted. She hated that when I came to visit, she would have to be in the office versus work from home every day, which she was doing. So, she didn't want me to visit to save her the twenty-minute commute to the office. She would also complain about hard-to-deal-with clients to me, likely thinking she was bonding with me through venting, when in fact she often pushed such difficult clients onto me to deal with.

After Kelly went on her leave of absence and Heather stepped in as our manager, Shannon's campaign against me escalated. If any client interactions were negative—not because of my customer service, but rather their difficult attitudes or dissatisfaction with my inability to accommodate unreasonable requests—Shannon would forward the emails to Heather without looping me in for context. She was very comfortable talking crap about how horrible these clients were, and even more comfortable throwing me under the bus. I didn't understand why Shannon was acting like a snake, but I later learned that it was because she wanted Anna, her friend and a rock star sales rep from another team, to step into my place.

If Heather had been a good manager, she would have approached me in an unbiased way to seek clarity. But because Shannon, the Southern belle with the sweet exterior, was more senior than me, Heather just took her word for everything and started making her lists of my "faults." She approached me with an attitude of correcting me versus seeking understanding. It felt like every week I was being called out for something new that was either taken completely out of context or entirely made up. From chastising me about my choice in hotel to telling me I could not work from home even though everyone else on our team only came in two to three times per week, I was being singled out. There were so-called "client complaints," which I requested copies of so I could read them for myself, but Heather denied me access to "protect the client." This went on for many weeks, until at last I was put on a dreaded "performance plan."

For most people, months of bad performance with concrete examples will get you put on a performance plan. For me, it was three weeks of a smear campaign by Heather and Shannon. There was no room to ask for clarity, and no way to respectfully push back. I just had to lay there while I was being kicked.

Have you ever been there? Even recalling these events makes me feel emotional. These women, without any reason beyond their own selfishness, made life a nightmare for me. Somehow, Shannon's word was considered final, even though she was only one level senior to me in the hierarchy. Heather had a great brand in the company and was known as a strong leader because of her ability to drive sales. She came off as the sarcastic, cool girl who could drink with the guys, so I don't blame people for liking her. Even I did … at first.

It quickly became clear that these two would be successful in pushing me out of the company. I didn't want to leave, so I got creative. I asked Heather to collect and share feedback from the wider team as part of my performance plan evaluation. The three other team members worked with me closely. We got along great, and I knew they would be honest about my successes and areas of improvement. I scheduled one-to-ones with each of them and was transparent about what was going on. They were shocked. When I shared some of the examples of criticism Heather and Shannon had about me and how situations were twisted to appear as if I was the problem, they quickly came to my defense, "That's not what happened!" they agreed. They confirmed I was great to work with and took pride in my work, basically opposing everything Shannon claimed. Heather approached these colleagues for feedback on me, but what she didn't know was that my colleagues bcc'd me on their responses. I saw every word of the feedback they shared with Heather. However, when it was time for Heather to share the feedback, she generalized very specific proof points and examples into, "They like you as a person, Devika." This was infuriating. I wanted to clap back and say, "Actually, no. What they shared with you was…" but I knew doing that would compromise my team. Why bring them into my mess? They didn't deserve that, so I kept my mouth shut.

The performance plan kept building with unfair and incorrect examples of how I was epically failing. "Devika's colleagues enjoy working with her because of her personality but had trouble highlighting strengths that are critical to the success of this role." Lies. It was a case built on bias and manipulation, and we all knew it.

I had one more lever to pull to save my job: vulnerability. I thought I could level with Heather. If she knew how much I loved my job and wanted to be there, maybe she would have some compassion and work with me instead of against me. Moreover, if I stroked her ego, maybe she'd lay off. So, I booked a one-to-one, and opened with, "Heather, I realize that the last few months have been a struggle. While I do not agree with some examples that have been shared, I'm focused on the solution and getting back to a good place. I love this company. I love my clients and my work. I love my colleagues. This is a place I want to grow. I'm committed to turning this around, but I need your support."

"You need my support?" Heather scoffed. "Devika, only you can help yourself. I've given you the areas you need to improve, but only you can do that. I'm not sure how I can support you."

"You're right, you have given me areas to focus on. But I feel when I ask for clarity or disagree with certain things, you call me defensive. If I try to provide context on a misunderstanding, I'm told I'm deflecting blame. Again, I want to turn this around and get to a better place in our relationship. I'm just asking for the space to ask questions or provide context from my perspective."

"Devika, what I've realized about you is that you will not take accountability. Here you are telling me you're committed to turning things around, but in the same breath asking to be able to explain yourself. Why can't you just take feedback? Feedback is a gift."

I was officially out of options. This was outright gaslighting. There was no reasoning with Heather.

My hair started falling out from stress, I couldn't sleep, and I had constant anxiety, something I had never experienced before, going into work every day. "I wonder what Heather has to say today about my shitty performance?" I'd ask myself.

My colleague and friend, Marlene, who was also the Executive Assistant to the Head of the Canadian office, took notice. "Devi, what's up, babe?" she asked, sitting down next to me. "You okay, girl?" I immediately started bawling right there at my desk. We quickly found a conference room so nobody would see me getting emotional. I told Marlene what was going on. She was shocked. She, too, had heard Heather was a strong manager, and her boss—the head of our department across North America—loved her.

"I'm surprised to hear this. I know you and I'm shocked to hear that she's going in on you like this. She sounds straight-up mean! But listen, Dev, you've got to take a beat for yourself. I know you, and this is not you. You need to take some time and get yourself right."

This was sound advice, and I have since passed it on to other underrepresented professionals who find themselves in unfair and stressful situations. Taking time off most certainly meant giving Heather the ammunition she needed to get rid of me—but by then, I was too tired to care. I couldn't continue to be this unhappy. It just wasn't me. I had allowed Heather and Shannon's sabotage to make me physically and emotionally sick, and it had to stop. So, I went to the doctor, explained what I was experiencing, and got a note to excuse me from work for three weeks. Of course, despite being on medical leave, those three weeks counted toward the four-week deadline I had been given to "turn things around" and keep my job. Basically, when I got back to work, I would have only had one week to prove I had made massive strides and appease Heather. This, of course, was totally unrealistic. When I presented Heather with the note and told her I'd be out for three weeks, she simply responded, "Okay." No concern for my well-being, not even a question as to why. I'm positive she thought I was playing games, but that didn't matter anymore.

Those three weeks gave me clarity. I slept, I meditated—and mostly, I prayed. "God, why are you letting this happen? I have worked diligently, always gave my all, and always showed love to people through kindness. Why am I being attacked?" I had thoughts of going to HR and bringing all of this to their attention, including a video I took at a team off-site on my Instagram when Heather (jokingly, but inappropriately) called me an idiot for leaving early instead of playing the next drinking game. They had to see I wasn't the problem here. But the feeling passed. It wasn't worth it. I simply had to accept that my glorious run at a company I loved and wanted to grow in was over. I balanced my memories of the great times I'd had at the company with regret that I had ever taken this new role. If I had stayed put with my former supportive team and manager instead of wanting to move up the ladder and gain new skills and compensation, I reasoned, I would still be thriving. But deep down, I knew that logic wasn't right. Despite my horrendous experience working with Heather and Shannon, I *had* developed new skills and business acumen, much of which still serves me today as an entrepreneur.

Once I realized I could not let these people steal my joy, I no longer felt like I needed to prove myself. It was over, and I was at peace. I used the remainder of my three weeks to decompress and strategize about how to approach Heather and the performance plan when I returned.

Of course, when I got back to work, there was a one-to-one meeting with Heather on my calendar. She jumped right into it. "There is one week left on your performance plan. You have made limited improvements and, with five business days remaining, we are tracking to move to a follow-up plan that will lead to termination if you can't get it together."

Depressed and anxious Devika was gone. In her place was accepting, calm, and collected Devika. Coolly, I responded, "Heather, I'm disappointed that after several years of performing well and having a great brand at this company that it's come to this. I don't want to use our time discussing who is right and who is wrong. At this point it's clear that you don't believe I belong here. I don't think it's necessary to move into another plan. If you're going to terminate me, I will gracefully accept it, but I'm not leaving on my own. I'd like to propose something that may work for both of us. We can agree that I will be terminated and agree on what will be my last day here? I also do not want to be escorted out like I've seen happen to other employees who were terminated. I've spent five years here cultivating friendships and respect with my peers and leaders. I'd like the opportunity to tell them that I no longer work here and leave in a way that honors my investment here. In exchange, I will write detailed notes on every account and transition them to whoever will be taking over. I will also use these two weeks to wrap up any pending initiatives for clients so they are confident when I leave. I'll leave the business buttoned up and in a great position for my replacement to take over."

Heather's demeanor changed in that moment. I think she assumed I'd be fighting my way through an eventual termination. Mostly, I think she was surprised by my cooperation. She accepted my proposal and acknowledged that I'd had a great run at the company. She said that, despite our differences, she didn't want to embarrass me, and thanked me for being "mature" about the situation.

Two weeks later, I had a farewell lunch with my team and sent out my goodbye email to the peers. Nobody knew I had been terminated. It appeared that my departure was on my terms—which, in reality, it was. Yes, I was pushed out, but I maneuvered it to work in my favor. By quitting before Heather could fire me, I was able to claim unemployment, which took the financial pressure off of me for a few months until I started my new job. I was also able to keep my health benefits for a longer period of time versus it being cut off immediately if I resigned. There was no possible way to explain to everyone what had happened and still protect my reputation and brand, so I exited on my own terms, and left it at that.

To this day, I don't believe Heather began with ill intent. Shannon's need to feel superior and manipulate situations to unfold in her favor was the root cause of my fate. It didn't begin with Heather—but Heather was determined, and when her mind was made up there was no seeking understanding or allowing for different perspectives. She was great with clients, an awesome communicator, and almost always got the team to hit our revenue goals, but she lacked grace, empathy, and leading in a fair way, which unfortunately aren't skills that are easily learned.

On my final day, Heather left me a voicemail to thank me for my time there. She also mentioned how much she adored me as a person and was disappointed that it ended that way. I wish I could say I appreciated the message, but I really didn't. We never spoke again, yet I often see her viewing my Instagram stories. A friend recently asked me why I still allow her to follow me. The answer is, I want her to see me shining. I want her to see that the experience she and Shannon put me through didn't break me. Instead, it worked in my favor.

After leaving the company, I took eight weeks off before starting in the new role I landed as a people manager on a sales team. I traveled solo to Israel, Amsterdam, and the Bahamas with zero shame, hurt, or anger. I felt free. I celebrated all my professional achievements up until that point and started to ask myself questions like, "What do I really want?" That one question would change the course of my professional career forever.

My new role was with an e-commerce startup in Toronto that was growing like crazy. I was hired to manage a sales team—a role that would enable me to become the kind of leader I wish I'd had as an individual contributor. The company was great, my team was awesome, my manager was cool, and I was making $50,000 more than in my previous role. This really seemed like an exciting next phase of my career—but within a few months, something in me just … switched. Even though everything was good, I felt this intense tugging in my spirit that said, "There's more for you." I loved sales and was good at it, but I was no longer thrilled by meeting a quota or selling solutions to clients. I wanted to help people, specifically underrepresented people, navigate the turbulent waters of their careers—and, the reality was, I was already doing it. In the decade I spent working in tech, I had mentored and supported dozens of people on how they should navigate challenges in their careers. As a founding member of the Black and Women's employee resource groups at Google and LinkedIn, I poured hours a week into sharing the advice, strategies, and frameworks that helped me take big leaps in my career and increase my compensation quickly. I wanted to keep doing that—but this time, as my career.

Before my experience with Heather and Shannon, I had never asked myself, "What do I want?" I simply followed the formula: climb the corporate ladder in globally known companies, make more money every year, and most importantly, make my single mom who sacrificed so much for me to have a bright and stable future proud. But now, looking at the future, I suddenly realized it wasn't enough. A corporate climb—even doing something I liked—wasn't how I wanted to spend my life. Driving revenue in my sales roles and fostering authentic relationships was my talent, but it wasn't my *purpose.*

This realization started to haunt me. I began feeling fatigued going into work every day. I felt mentally fuzzy and emotionally dissatisfied, and I knew it wasn't going to change. I would call my mom from the food court of my office building and vent to her that I wasn't in the right place and didn't know what to do. I'd worked so hard for this job, and it was still new. Perhaps I was still dealing with grief over losing my place in my former company.

My mom listened, but instead of encouraging me to stay, she said, "You need to pray about this. I know you'll make the right decision."

So, I prayed. I waited for my situation to change and for peace in the change to arrive, but it didn't. The thought of leaving my new job without any backup plan was crippling, but that path also brought me the most peace. I had a deep knowing that, although this choice made no sense, I would be okay. I needed to give myself the chance to figure out what was truly for me, and what was not. So, a few short months into my new role, I pulled my manager aside and said I couldn't stay. I told him, "I love it here, and I love my team, but I can't effectively manage this team and fulfill my responsibilities if my heart isn't in it. I want to thank you so much for choosing me for this role, and I'm sorry to let you down."

He was shocked and confused and tried to understand what he needed to provide for me to stay. Realizing there wasn't anything he could say or do, he wished me well and sent me on my way.

I remember getting back to my apartment that day at 11:00 a.m. with absolutely nothing to do and nowhere to be, and thinking to myself, "What have you done?" But the question was not met with fear; it was met with an overwhelming peace.

My unemployment lasted over a year. Thankfully I had been saving up for a down payment on a midtown Toronto condo, so I had funds set aside that could get me through this transition time. For the first time in my life, I focused on *me*. I rested, enjoyed not being on multiple planes a week for client meetings, processed my experience with Heather and other unfair situations in my corporate career, invested in my health, and … I just got right.

During that year, I kept getting calls from previous colleagues who needed advice about challenges they were facing at work or how they should approach intimidating conversations with their leaders. Then, I started to receive calls from people who were referred to me by others. I began charging hourly fees for coaching calls, and developed workshops that presented solutions for the challenges my clients were facing. A few months later, I met Brittany, a Learning and Development Professional at Facebook (now Meta). I pitched a program that I had developed that paired career advancement content, coaching, and community to help people of color and women thrive in their careers. She loved it, and a few months later, I landed my first corporate client! Slowly, I began adding other corporate clients to my roster through sharing success stories of my program. Today, Brij the Gap is a successful career and leadership development consulting firm.

Despite the success of my new venture, you will never hear me take credit for what my career has transformed into. I believe this alignment and mission could only come into fruition by God, through faith. Everything was perfectly orchestrated to get me here. In fact, if my experience with Shannon and Heather never occurred, I can confidently say I'd still be at that company, doing work that I liked but that didn't ultimately fulfill me. Before I knew that there was something bigger for me to accomplish, God knew. Every challenge I navigated in the workplace as a person of color enabled me to help others navigate theirs—and, as a community, we overcame together. Not a day goes by that I don't look back and remember where I came from.

I'm so grateful. For *all* of it.

WHAT DO YOU WANT?

Now, it's time to ask yourself that career-shifting question: "What do you really want?"

This is a question that most underrepresented professionals never ask themselves. For most, exploring options versus chasing what we believe qualifies "success" is not an opportunity that has ever been encouraged. It will probably make you uncomfortable, and that's okay. Sit with the question, and know that there is no right or wrong answer. You may realize that you are indeed on the path you want to pursue, or that you're so far off track that you feel lost in a fog. You may realize that the corporate climb is what you desire, and that you love the structure and security that working for a company gives you. You may want to pursue another job function or seniority level. You may be driven by money and want to continue on your path to keep increasing your compensation. Or, like me, you may realize that your end goal is to move into entrepreneurship.

If you sit with this question and realize that you're generally satisfied and want to continue the career trajectory you're on and achieve the most you possibly can, this book has given you many key strategies to refine your path for greater success.

On the other hand, if your spirit is guiding you to explore leaving your role, your company, or even your industry, let's talk about your exit strategy.

KNOW WHEN TO LEAVE

A question I often get from clients, regardless of whether they are both satisfied in their careers, is, "How do I know when to leave?"

Deciding when to leave your job can be confusing and even emotional, especially if you still enjoy the company, team, or manager you work with. Knowing whether your advancement and development goals have hit a wall, or if there is still room for growth if you just wait it out, can be difficult. That's why it's essential to give yourself time to make a well-considered decision, and to trust your gut.

Although some of my clients have been with their companies for thirty years or more, for most professionals today the average time spent within a role is two to four years. While moving from opportunity to opportunity was once a red flag on resumes, companies now realize that employees are switching roles and companies more rapidly than ever before to take advantage of perks and incentives as the space has become increasingly competitive. While increasing retention is top-of-mind for most employers, most companies have not embraced the experiences and structures they *must* provide to retain top talent and turn them into future leaders in the company. Therefore, it's up to you to take care of yourself, and know when it's time to go.

Here are some factors that may indicate that it's time to move on to your next role (or to another company altogether).

Impact to Your Well-Being

If you are dealing with a toxic workplace and leadership team, unsupportive peers, unfair treatment where you're singled out or held back, discrimination, harassment, burnout, or anything else that affects your mental and/or physical well-being and hinders your career growth, it's time to exit. If you have communicated these factors to your manager, HR, or other leaders in your organization but the company has not taken proactive steps to address these issues and offer support, they have shown you that they do not prioritize your well-being, so why continue to invest in them?

Lack of Career Advancement

If you've asked for development and advancement opportunities through proving your contributions and consistently driving exposure to your accomplishments, but the company never seems to have headcount or budget for the role you are ready for, or the goalposts keep moving every time you get close to a promotion, that's a good indication that it's time to explore other options. Lack of mobility within companies isn't always intentional—tough economies, budget cuts, layoffs, and hiring freezes are common realities that may impact your ability to receive advancement opportunities—but if you're craving opportunities to advance, apply your skills, and make more income, you would be doing yourself a disservice by continuing to wait for things to change. Let's also be real: it's possible that your workplace *can* provide advancement opportunities, but you're being intentionally held back and kept in a cycle that makes you believe your time is coming soon. Whatever the situation is, it's important for you to set and communicate clear boundaries around what you need, what you're ready for, and how long you're willing to wait for your employer to create the path or incentive you're looking for. You are the decision-maker here, so put yourself first and make decisions that will make you feel empowered and successful both today and in the longer term.

Consistent Unhappiness

If your work lacks the challenge and interest it once had, or the environment causes you to dread going to work every day, it will start to take a serious toll on your emotional, physical, and mental well-being. It's common to have seasons of not feeling motivated and wanting more, but if you're not re-energized by taking on new projects or incentives, it's time to look at alternatives.

Lifestyle Change

Perhaps you've purchased a new home, are growing your family, are going back to school, have taken on the care of your parents, are dealing with other life-changing events, or have simply gotten sick of being underpaid. If your compensation doesn't support the lifestyle you want, it's perfectly acceptable to find another role that will meet your salary requirements. Remember, we work to live, not live to work.

Misalignment in Values

The company you work for, whether you believe it or not, is a representation of you. If you don't agree with the company's core values, their culture, or how they treat their clients and members, it's better to go somewhere you feel proud to be. Conversely, some of my clients have gone through seasons of feeling uninspired or hitting a wall in their roles, but their deep connection to the company's mission and values ultimately kept them motivated. Where you work matters, and you should feel connected to the greater purpose of your role or the company. Is it okay to take a job solely for the experience and skill development? Absolutely. But your larger goal should be to work for a company you feel connected to, because that larger sense of purpose will keep you engaged and feeling productive.

***

Now that we've talked about environments you should absolutely exit because they are not serving you, allow me to highlight scenarios that are *not* a reason to leave your current role.

Self-Inflicted Expectations

Some professionals begin experiencing 3D feelings because they have not been able to advance their careers within the timeline they identified for themselves.

My client, AJ, was obsessed with his job, but as soon as he'd been in the role for twelve months, his energy and motivation tanked. He said, "I've been in the role for a year now, so it's time to move forward, but my manager says there's no opportunity for me to move right now. Can we schedule some time to talk about my resume and interview preparation?" AJ's impatience had him ready to leave all the momentum he had built in the last twelve months!

"I'm happy to pivot our conversations if needed," I told him, "but are you sure this role is no longer the right fit?"

AJ explained that he was happy with his work, his manager, and his team, but if there were no growth opportunities available right now, it was time to move on. AJ had opportunities to mold his role to gain the experience and skills he felt he needed to develop. His leadership team loved him and were willing to help him move up in the organization, but at that exact moment, they were going through a re-org, and decisions like promotion, salary increases, and other incentives were on hold until the new structure of the company was established.

To AJ, this reality didn't matter. He was on his own timeline and was driving full force to meet his personal timelines.

Once I helped AJ to unpack his reasoning for this choice, I learned that he was fearful of employers taking advantage of his talent and keeping him around to squeeze everything out of him before they ultimately told him they couldn't offer him what he needed to stay. While this is a reality I help my clients look out for, it truly did not seem as though his managers were misleading him. So, I helped AJ gain the answers he needed from his managers and set realistic expectations around the growth opportunities he desired. He then was able to direct his energy to learning as much as he could in his current role—and, within a few months, he was promoted into the role he desired. The time he spent developing his skill set helped him tremendously in his new job.

If you've exhausted all options in your workplace and you're truly ready to move forward, go for it! But, if you're leaving simply because the timelines you've given yourself aren't working out the way you thought, I'd advise you to reconsider. Leaving a job because you haven't received a promotion or raise in a short amount of time is likely due to impatience and unrealistic expectations that can actually harm your growth. Career advancement takes time, and while you absolutely do not want a company to take advantage of your great work with no plan to advance or reward you, it's essential to consider the ways you're growing in your current role that will serve you in the future, instead of looking only at the immediate rewards.

Expecting Perfection

No job is perfect. Most of the time, even if you love your job, about 20 percent of your work will be boring, challenging, and outright annoying. Leaving a job to escape challenges, difficult projects, difficult people, or a learning curve can seriously hinder your professional growth. Overcoming challenges is necessary for career and character development.

Short-Term Frustration

Leaving a job during a short-term period of frustration or dissatisfaction without giving yourself adequate time to assess and resolve the issues may result in missed opportunities for improvement. It's okay to feel bored, demotivated, dissatisfied with your leadership team or organizational changes, and irritated with personality conflicts, but it's important to not let those feelings consume you.

Feelings are exactly that: feelings. They come, they go, they change. Making decisions that impact your life and livelihood based on short-term frustration without allowing yourself adequate time to assess the situation and possibly turn it around will harm you more than help.

***

Before you leave your job, carefully evaluate your motivations, the potential consequences of your decision, and your long-term career goals. Hopefully this chapter has given you more perspective around whether you're exiting early or right on time.

I also encourage you to talk with a trusted mentor, career coach, or leader to gain feedback and support if you are considering leaving your job. Often, discussing this decision with a trusted party can reveal a perspective that you're not considering (like I was able to do for AJ). That said, remember that you are in the driver's seat of your career, and only you can assess whether you're being intentionally held back or whether a bit more time and patience will get you what you desire. Trust your intuition, your gut, and your spirit, and take the time to evaluate your needs and motivations before you make decisions.

LEADING AND LEAVING WITH GRACE

When I was negotiating my departure and termination from the company I loved so dearly, some of my friends and peers were shocked.

"Devika, how are you doing this? How can you let your manager treat you like that and then agree to make her life easier? If you know she's going to terminate you, why put in the effort?"

My peers were angry for me and being protective. Also, they weren't wrong. Most people would not orchestrate a graceful exit and set their replacement up for success after being bullied and essentially forced out for no reason. I realized that I had the power to royally screw over Heather in retaliation for her unfair treatment of me. But I didn't want to. One of my values is respect for others—and I live by that value whether others acknowledge me for it or not. Whether I was being disrespected and degraded was not my focus. It hurt, yes. Shit, it *still* hurts when I think back on it, but I didn't want my actions to make Heather's lies about me true. Nor did I want to give her the satisfaction of thinking she got rid of a bad seed on the team. She was wrong, and although I didn't have the energy or desire (or ability, really) to convince her through my words, I knew she would see it through the grace I offered her.

I had spent years building my professional brand at the company. I had phenomenal relationships with my peers, my clients, and many senior leaders. To allow those last few months of harsh treatment to jeopardize all that I had built would have been foolish. I might have been pushed out of the company, but I would never act in a way where my character would be questioned.

So, I completed my projects and pending tasks with my accounts, ensured my clients were set up for success, and wrote detailed client notes so the person replacing me could step in with minimal assimilation time. And, in the end, I left feeling good about myself.

When I tell this story to clients and partners, the most common question that comes up is, "What happened to Shannon and Heather?"

The short story is that Shannon ended up leaving the company two weeks before I did, while I was out on leave. Suddenly and without warning, she decided to take a job in London to be closer to her Parisian boyfriend. I often wonder why she felt the need to throw me under the bus if her goal was to leave anyway. I'll never have the answer—but Anna, the friend she wanted in my role, did end up taking over my position.

Heather left the company two weeks after my last day. I later found out that, while she was making my life at work miserable every day for months, she was interviewing for other roles, and ended up taking a position at a company that went under a year later. Apparently, her desire to leave was prompted by the fact that she wasn't being promoted into a Director role at our company, even though she was operating in that role while Kelly, my previous manager, was on leave. Looking back, I realize that Heather may have been taking out her anger and frustration on me. Perhaps she even used me as an example to her new employers of how she acted to "correct" problematic people on the team. It hardly matters now, because although the whole experience was traumatic, I wouldn't be here, writing these words to you, without it.

All drama aside, here's my final piece of advice to you with regard to exiting a role for any reason.

Rather than retaliating, quiet quitting, or storming out in anger (even if it's fully warranted), keep your eye on your goals. In unfair situations, lean into your professional brand, values, and kindness. Lead with grace and prove them wrong with your class and dignity.

Leaving a company with grace allows you to be seen as a mature professional, and is also a valuable practice for maintaining positive relationships with your peers and leaders. The business world is a much smaller place than we might think, and it's highly likely you could cross paths with former peers and leaders in future companies or discover that mutual connections from your past are connected to people in your future. So, show up in the best way you can, all the way to your exit.

Here are the steps to leaving your company with grace.

Provide Sufficient Notice

If you're leaving on your own terms and in good standing with the company, you should provide at least two weeks' notice to your manager and team so they can reassign your responsibilities and gain your insights before your departure. If you are leaving of your own will because the environment is no longer pleasant or you are being actively held back from advancement, I still suggest giving at least one week's notice. Even if you're leaving on not-so-good terms, giving adequate notice shows that you are thoughtful, considerate, and professional.

That said, if your safety and health is at risk, there are ethical challenges, or the workplace has become hostile or toxic, staying for two extra weeks is an unnecessary risk.

Practice Considerate Communication

If possible, schedule a quick in-person meeting with your manager to deliver the news of your departure. This is the most respectful way of leaving the company. If in-person is not possible, a video call is the next best option, followed by an audio call. Delivering the news of your resignation via email, text, or internal chat message can feel blindsiding and inconsiderate.

If you're feeling animosity toward your manager or employer, you may be thinking, "Who cares if I blindside them? They deserve it." Remember, this is not about retaliation; rather, this is an opportunity to respectfully show them that they are losing a professional and considerate asset to the team.

Prepare for Your Transition

Offer assistance in training your replacement to ensure a smooth handover of your responsibilities. Also be sure to document pending projects and specific processes around how you manage your work to support whoever is taking over your workload.

Share Your Feedback

If you have the chance to participate in an exit interview, communicate areas of improvement for the company and the leadership team constructively. You should absolutely be transparent about your experiences and suggest what you would have liked to have seen done differently, but keep the feedback focused on facts versus emotions.

Express Gratitude

Take a moment to thank the peers, mentors, sponsors, and colleagues who made your time at the company memorable. A handwritten card always goes a long way. Even if your experience wasn't ideal, saying something like, "I'm grateful for the experience working with the team (or company)" conveys a mature attitude, even if it isn't relevant to all parties.

There is always something to be thankful for, even in the most challenging and frustrating situations. In my encounter with Heather before leaving, I expressed gratitude for her willingness to allow me to leave with dignity so I wouldn't feel embarrassed, despite the fact that her treatment of me was wrong. Don't allow anyone to make you feel small. Expressing gratitude makes you the bigger person, always.

Maintain Your Connections

Make it a point to stay in touch with colleagues and professional contacts whom you got along with and collaborated with effectively. You never know when your paths may cross again. You may be able to leverage their feedback for future referrals or LinkedIn recommendations when looking for your next opportunity. Just be sure to reciprocate if they ask!

***

How you leave a company can have an impact on your reputation, personal brand, and future job prospects, so it's essential to maintain professionalism and courtesy throughout the process. The company you're leaving is losing a great asset—*you*. The manner in which you leave will make them recognize that.

As we've discussed throughout this book, you cannot avoid situations where you deserve to be elevated and instead find yourself having to pivot and pursue alternative paths. You cannot prevent people who haven't worked through their own insecurities and biases from treating you poorly. But you can, always, control what you bring to the table. Your actions always have the final say.

Chapter Thirteen

THRIVE IN COLOR

THROUGHOUT THIS BOOK, we've discussed tools and strategies that will help you win across every season of your professional journey. However, I realize that adopting all these strategies can feel overwhelming. At this point, you may be feeling motivated yet unsure of where to start.

If you frantically implement all that you've learned in this book, the changes you make will likely be impactful, but may also feel forced. Your managers and leaders may also feel thrown off if you come in full swing with major shifts. Ideally, you want your approach to career development, advancement, and growth to feel organic. Career advancement takes time and should be nurtured. My desire for you is not to completely rewrite the script all at once, but rather to feel a consistent peace throughout your career journey, even when you're experiencing challenges.

So, I want you to take a deep breath and relax. You have all the time you need to put these strategies and tools to work in your career. You'll get there. Eventually, self-advocacy will become not a strategy or action step, but a way of life.

To make this transition into owning your narrative and practicing effective self-advocacy easier and more natural for you, I'm going to give you the exact first steps to reset and relaunch your approach to career development and advancement. These will provide big impact and clarity right away, without overwhelming you. After that, you can go back and implement the rest of the strategies you've learned when you feel comfortable or as they become relevant to your career journey.

YOUR FIRST STEPS TO THRIVE IN COLOR

Establish Regular One-to-Ones and Career Check-In Conversations

In Chapters Nine and Ten, we talked about the importance of elevating your contributions and accomplishments through consistent one-to-ones, and of having regular career check-ins so you always know where you stand.

If you are not having consistent one-to-one meetings with your manager or they always get rescheduled or canceled, your first step is to get a standing weekly or biweekly meeting on the calendar. No matter how well you perform or how much you accomplish, it means nothing if you aren't driving exposure to your contributions. Remember, 60 percent of your career success is dependent on self-advocacy, and there is no better environment to drive visibility to your work than one-to-one meetings with your manager. Remember, this should be a mutually beneficial conversation that enables your manager to receive the information they need from you while you highlight your great work, ask questions, and seek feedback around whatever is top-of-mind for you.

One-to-one meetings and career check-ins are not "nice to haves." They are critical. In fact, if you only implement a single strategy from this book, it should be to get those meetings on the calendar. When you navigate these meetings the way I've taught you, you will notice a game-changing shift in how you approach, communicate with, and partner with leaders in your career.

Develop Your Executive Summary & CISS

As an underrepresented professional, you should never allow anyone to create a narrative about you based on their perception of you.

Your performance in your career will go through seasons of highs and lows. You'll likely be surprised at who goes from calling you a "superstar" one minute to "not a good fit" the next. That's why it's important that you create and drive your reputation, the areas of strength you want to be known for, and how people describe you.

Your first steps in creating and scaling your professional brand are to understand what makes you unique, what matters to you, and your specific contributions. In Chapter Five, I introduced the CISS Framework which will help you establish the foundations of your professional brand. When you have an understanding of who you are as a professional, and most importantly as an entire individual, you'll be equipped to directly and indirectly guide your colleagues and leaders around how to view you and describe you.

Your executive summary, which we explored in Chapter Seven, comes next. I can promise you, the first draft will be challenging to create—I've never heard anyone I've taught this framework to describe it as easy—but don't let the challenge intimidate you. After you have a solid version of your headline and leadership, scaling solutions, and results examples, put your executive summary away for a few days and then revisit it again. If you feel good about how it looks, share it with your leader in your next one-to-one, career check-in conversation, or performance review. The executive summary will always be an effective way to communicate your success and accomplishments and build a case for advancement, so make sure to spend quality time here and lean into the challenge of creating your first version. I promise, every time you revise, optimize, or add to your executive summary, it will get easier and more intuitive.

Cultivate Your Network of Advocates

In Chapter Eight, you learned the importance of cultivating a network of advocates who will support you through your development and advancement goals. After you set up one-to-ones and career check-ins with your leader and create your CISS Framework and executive summary, it's time to reach out and begin building a trusted group of individuals who will guide and champion you for opportunities.

We identified the three categories of people to have in your network of advocates as mentors, sponsors, and career allies. However, at this stage of your journey, I want you to prioritize securing at least one sponsor. Over time, you can continue to add additional people like mentors and career allies to your network, but sponsors are generally the most impactful in the short term—

particularly sponsors in leadership positions who have influence over decision-makers. Focus your initial efforts on getting at least one, if not two, engaged sponsors who are committed to elevating and championing you.

Know What You Want

The final item in your list of immediate priorities is completing the career brainstorm chart I shared in Chapter Eleven. Getting crystal clear about your career advancement desires is important so you know what to advocate for. You cannot be vague about your desires, assume your manager can read your mind, or expect leadership to come up with rewards and incentives for you. You should know what you want and what you're asking for at all times.

Whether you're ready to negotiate for your growth or advancement goals right now or not, it's important to be prepared if your leader asks you what you need or want to feel successful within the company. Having an answer prepared for both planned and unplanned conversations about your career desires shows that you are thinking long term. So, take some time to prepare your ideal, exceptional, and great (A, B, and C) options. If you're happy with where you are at or new to your company or role, I encourage you to think about the skills you want to develop or the future role you are working toward and create options around resources that will help get you there.

***

After you've nailed down the four immediate priorities above, come back to each chapter and slowly begin implementing the rest of the tools and recommendations. Remember, career development and advancement take time. Trying to do everything at once leads to burnout and discouragement rather than success—but small, intentional steps will take you a long way. If you're feeling motivated to reset, refine, and recharge your career through the actions you learned in this playbook, I couldn't be happier. Just do it in the way that feels best to you—because at the end of the day, this work is *all about you.*

Your success means so much to me.

I'm rooting for you.

Afterword

IN 2015, I ATTENDED a career development seminar in Toronto. The speakers were impressive female leaders who were known as the best in their fields.

I was there to see a specific person, who I won't name. This woman was bold, confident, and had held C-level roles at some of the world's most notable brands. She would spend short periods of time at each company building her skills and contributions, and gained a lot of media coverage for being one of only a few Black women in the C-suite. I appreciated her success and also loved her vibe. She inspired me to bring my full self to work every day.

I listened from the audience as the event host asked question after question on how women in corporate can climb the ladder as effectively as this leader did. However, as accomplished, funny, fabulous, and charismatic as she was, I couldn't help but feel disappointed in her answers. Why? Because nothing she was saying was tangible. Sure, it was motivational, and I felt inspired by her journey, but I wanted the "how-to" behind it all. I wanted the playbook, and she didn't provide it. I left feeling like I could have gotten so much more from the experience than I had—and I'm sure I wasn't the only woman of color in the audience who felt that way.

I attended many more of these conferences over the years. I read books and listened to hundreds of interviews. Over time, I realized this was a common gap in what were supposed to be supportive resources for underrepresented professionals. The "how-to" just wasn't available. I would feel inspired and motivated while consuming these resources, but ultimately lacked clear steps to follow when it was time to execute. So, I had to create them for myself.

The steps for self-advocacy that you've learned in this book is the product of years of research, trial and error, and outright failing (both forward and backward). It includes the learnings from the greatest leaps and bounds in my career, as well as the wisdom of my biggest mess-ups. More, it includes the feedback and results of the thousands of clients who created amazing results with the tools I've provided.

I'll be honest: writing this book has been one of the most challenging endeavors I've ever taken on. The thing is, I never desired to write a book or be an author. My desire was to help people—to help *you*—win. I wanted to provide the "how-to" that was missing from the hundreds of resources I'd consumed in search of answers. And, while I spend my days helping underrepresented professionals with career development and advancement through my partnerships with corporations, I realize that not everyone works for a company that will pay for and offer career development programs. I realize that access to conferences and personal coaches isn't always an option. That's why I knew I needed to write this book—because no matter what company you work for or where you are in your career, you deserve to know the how-to of professional self-advocacy and commanding the career you deserve.

Whether you are new in your career or a few years away from retirement, it's never too early or late to create the career you desire. You spend way too much of your time at work to have a mediocre or challenging experience. You deserve to feel fulfilled and proud of the work that you're doing, and to be rewarded and incentivized. But—as I've shared from the beginning—it all starts with you.

I've received pushback in the past from other underrepresented professionals for saying things like, "You're in the driver's seat of your career." But I've said it throughout this book, and I'll keep saying it. I've shared my stories, and those of some of my clients, with regard to adversity and unfair treatment in the workplace—but you don't need me to tell you what we, as underrepresented professionals, are up against. It's extremely difficult to not let workplace challenges get to you. But that's exactly why making the choice to thrive is so critical to your success. We cannot control the unfair behaviors and systems that are designed to hold us back in the workplace and in society at large. However, we can always control what we bring to the table as unique individuals, and make the choices that benefit us in each situation, even if that means walking away with our head held high.

I can't promise you that your path and experiences will be easy, or that you won't run into challenges. But I *can* promise that if you put your full intention into moving strategically in your career, building your personal brand, and maintaining your momentum, you will attain experiences and fulfillment that once felt far beyond reach. The process to achieving a career that gets more fulfilling with time is continuous. As a constantly evolving human being whose interest, skills, experience, boundaries, priorities, and desires will change over the course of your career, there is no finish line. The secret to getting the results you want in your career is to implement the strategies you've learned in this book, adopt additional methods you learn from people you admire throughout your journey, and never stop making improvements.

Now that I've given you the playbook for how to navigate adversity and create career success, may I ask you something? Please pay it forward to your peers, family members, friends, mentees, children, siblings, and other people in your community who are struggling in their career or wanting more in their professional lives. Share the knowledge, tools, and strategies you have learned throughout this book, and support others to implement them. Introduce this book to your ERG, core team, or manager. Buy a copy for a friend. Be a mentor or a sponsor if you are in a position to do so. Be the resource you wish you had when you were younger.

As a child, I loved spending summer days in the swimming pool. Growing up with a single mom, I didn't experience family vacations in new destinations, but I always had the community swimming pool. I'd sprint toward the pool and jump, wrapping my arms around my knees to cannonball into the water. Waves would radiate throughout the pool in wide circles, touching everyone else in the pool. My hope and prayer is that, as you jump into these strategies and begin to generate success, the people around you—especially other professionals from marginalized communities—will catch the ripple effects of your victories. The only way we can create impact and change at scale, especially for communities of color, is to share our knowledge and steps to success with one another.

I'm so proud of you for making the decision to journey with me through the strategies and tools I've shared in this book. But now, as we wrap up our time together, you have a choice to make. You can either throw this book on your shelf to collect dust, and say, "I'll do this later when I feel more confident/prepared." Or, you can put aside your hesitations and actually execute on the proven frameworks you have access to right now. Athletes do not win simply by reviewing the playbook; they must go out there and put what they've learned into practice. You are worthy of having the career you desire, but only you can decide to embrace your full potential, slide into the driver's seat of your career, and be the change you want to see in your company, family, community, industry, or country.

I'm so excited for you to walk into a more empowered, successful, and fulfilled career, and I look forward to hearing the multiple success stories I am certain will evolve from choosing to invest in yourself. If you feel called, please share your success story with me on LinkedIn and tag me @devikabrij!

Thank you for allowing me to be a part of your career journey.

With love and belief in you,
Devika

Resources

To download the resources listed in this book,
go to **www.devikabrij.com/thriveincolor**

To learn more about Devika's work with corporations,
go to **www.brijthegapconsulting.com**

To book Devika to speak,
go to **www.devikabrij.com/speaking**

Acknowledgments

EVERYTHING I'VE BEEN able to overcome and accomplish is through the love and strength of Jesus Christ. It's only through Him that I get to do this meaningful work, and there's never a day when I forget it. He will always be the first to receive my gratitude and praise.

To my mom: when I left my safe, great-paying, corporate job to seek something "bigger" that I felt called to without knowing what that meant or having a plan, you encouraged my decision and believed in a vision that hadn't manifested yet. As an immigrant and single parent who sacrificed so much so your girls could have better opportunities, you could have convinced me to take the safe and predictable path but you trusted me as I pursued entrepreneurship to do more meaningful work. Your support has given me the confidence to reach beyond what I could ever have imagined for myself. Thank you.

To my husband and best friend, Greg. Your faith in me and our shared love for helping underserved individuals fill me with the daily energy I need to do this pivotal work. From processing ideas with me, to pouring me a glass of red during late-night writing sessions, and everything in between, thank you for being right by my side through this entire process.

To my sisters, Roseleen and Ang, and my sister-friends, who have been my biggest cheerleaders: your encouragement has lifted me up more than you know.

To my publishing team, and specifically, Bryna Haynes: thank you for being an intentional believer in my mission. Your support has gone above and beyond the call of duty.

To my corporate partners who continue to invest in underrepresented talent and trust me to develop them, your confidence in me has helped grow Brij the Gap Consulting to a leading learning and development company. Thank you for your support.

And finally, to every underrepresented professional I've had the opportunity to guide through coaching, programs and workshops, I celebrate you.

About the Author

DEVIKA BRIJ, CEO and Founder of Brij the Gap Consulting, is a champion and community builder for underrepresented individuals. She has over twelve years of experience in creating professional development frameworks and environments that enable underrepresented professionals to thrive.

Devika's path to becoming an expert in career and leadership development began with her own experiences as a woman of color navigating the barriers of advancing in corporate environments. Despite her consistent achievements and contributions, Devika was often overlooked for incentives and growth opportunities, causing her to feel unworthy of the career she desired. Instead of being defeated by the systems that were not designed for professionals of color to thrive, she created successful frameworks that would enable her, her peers, and the people she managed to attain the careers they deserved. After over a decade of working within Fortune 50 corporations like Google and LinkedIn, Devika launched Brij the Gap Consulting to help professionals of color apply strategy to career development and help companies unlock the potential of their underrepresented workforce.

Today, Devika spends her days partnering with Fortune 500 companies like Visa, Meta, Boston Consulting Group, Morgan Stanley, Saks, Glassdoor, and many more to increase retention of top talent and teach their underrepresented employees and leaders how to thrive in their careers.

Outside of her role as CEO of Brij the Gap, Devika is the Co-Founder of Zaka, a professional development platform that enables first and second generation immigrants to receive career advancement education, coaching, and community so they can win professionally.

Connect with Devika

www.devikabrij.com
www.brijthegapconsulting.com
www.zakaconnect.com

@devikabrij

@devikabrij

@brijthegapdevika

About the Publisher

FOUNDED IN 2021 by Bryna Haynes, WorldChangers Media is a boutique publishing company focused on "Ideas for Impact." We know that great books change lives, topple outdated paradigms, and build movements. Our commitment is to deliver superior-quality transformational nonfiction by, and for, the next generation of thought leaders.

Ready to write and publish your thought leadership book? Learn more at www.WorldChangers.Media.